THE RIVERSIDE COLLECTION
of Poetry

Also by Stanley Oliver:

Report Writing For Supervisors
(Bell and Sons Ltd)
O and M for First-Line Managers
(Edward Arnold Publishers)
Accountants Guide to Management Techniques
(Gower Press Ltd)
Case Studies (Bell and Sons Ltd)
The Management of Production Technology
(MEP Ltd)

THE RIVERSIDE COLLECTION

of Poetry

Stanley Oliver

The Book Guild Ltd

Sussex, England

The Book Guild Ltd.
25 High Street,
Lewes, Sussex

First Published 1992
© Stanley Oliver 1992
Set in Palatino
Typesetting by Ashford Setting and Design
Ashford, Middlesex
Printed in Great Britain by
Antony Rowe Ltd.
Chippenham, Wiltshire.

A catalogue record for this book is available from the British Library.

ISBN 0 86332 677 3

CONTENTS

PREFACE

The Shorter Oxford English Dictionary explains poetry as a composition in verse or metrical language. It is the expression of beautiful or elevated thought, imagination, or feeling, in appropriate language, such language containing a rhythmical element and having usually a metrical form. A poet is described as a writer in verse (or sometimes elevated prose) distinguished by imaginative power, insight, sensibility, and faculty of expression.

An early commentator is reputed to have said that 'To live poetry indeed, is always better than to write it'. Be that as it may, perhaps the most concise definition of poetry is attributable to Gwendolyn Brooks, the American poet, who said that 'Poetry is life distilled'.

The Spanish poet Juan Ramon Jimenez is reputed to have said that 'Literature is a state of culture, poetry is a state of grace', and the Russian poet Denise Levertov delves deeper, as follows:

'The poem has a social effect of some kind whether or not the poet wills that it have. It has a kinetic force, it sets in motion ... elements in the reader (listener) that otherwise would be stagnant'. Dylan Thomas would, I feel sure, agree with this.

Speaking for myself, I can only embark upon a creative expression through powerful emotional inspiration. I don't know if we have a word to explain this strongly enough but the Spanish have the word *'Duende'*, which is explained in my Spanish dictionary as 'elf, goblin or ghost'.

A contemporary of Federico García Lorca referred to the *duende* (the magic) of his personality, acting like electricity or a spell,' an irresistible atmosphere of magic which surrounded and captivated his audiences'.

Lorca believed that the poet needs to share laughter and tears with the people, and to deal directly with the themes of love, sorrow and death. Indeed, Lorca considered that in poetry, the *duende* is linked with the fact (the acceptance) of death. In summary, the *duende* is not to be taken in the limited form of definition as 'ghostly spirit', but as a creative life-stimulating spirit.

Lorca thought that the *duende* enters a person and establishes a lifelong struggle. In his view, this necessary struggle results in great artistic achievements.

All this makes it clear that the poet does not simply 'wait for inspiration'. '*Duende*-possession' (it seems to me) is more a matter of constant tuning to the fundamental life forces.

Lorca felt that a poem's magical quality consists in being possessed by the *duende*. By necessary implication, this means that it is easier to love and to understand, and to be loved and understood. The force of logic here is implied in the association of *duende* with the universally-felt life forces. So we overcome the apparent (and false) paradox that the awareness of death in our art forms serves to intensify our respect for life, in all its manifestations. Lorca, in his struggle to explain the *duende* fully, talks of 'the constant baptism of newly created things'.

Having thus established the source of my writing, it is of course important to mention the influence of other writers. I had the good fortune to attend a Grammar School where English Language and Literature were taught by enthusiasts and we were introduced to the English essayists and to Shakespeare and our 'founding poets', from the first year.

The influence of this must have been profound, as I can remember large portions of verse from those days whilst I remember little of my own recent verse! It was a liberation, the first contact with *duende*, perhaps? A contemporary American poet (Hart Crane) wrote, in 'The Broken Tower':

> 'And so it was I entered the broken world
> To trace the visionary company of love, its voice
> An instant in the wind (I know not whither hurled)
> But not for long to hold each desperate choice'

Of course the wind plays an important part in the *duende*. In Lorca's Canción we have the lines:

> '*El viento, galán de torres,*
> *La prendre por la cintura*'

being translated as:-

> 'The wind, that suitor of towers,
> takes her by the waist'

The girl in the field, after ignoring three invitations to accompany passing men to Cordoba, Seville or Granada:

> 'goes on gathering olives, with the grey arm
> of the wind encircling her waist'.

I suppose that I shall always be under the spells of Keats, Shakespeare and Dylan Thomas.

Shakespeare's direct simplicity attracts at once:-

'Where the bee sucks, there suck I;
In the cowslip's bell I lie:
There I couch when owls do cry.
On the bat's back I do fly
After Summer merrily:
Merrily, merrily shall I live now,
Under the blossom that hangs on the bough'
(Ariel: *The Tempest*, Act V Scene 1)

And Dylan Thomas's magic in 'Poem in October':

'A springful of larks in a rolling
Cloud and the roadside bushes brimming
with whistling
Blackbirds and the Sun of October
Summery
On the hill's shoulder'

Perhaps, at school, it was Keats ('a great spirit')
who cut the strongest into my developing mind?
Time only allowed reading of some of his major
poems at school, but later such gems as this came
into my reading and must surely stem from the
duende:

'I stood tip-toe upon a little hill,
The air was cooling, and so very still,
That the sweet buds which with a modest
pride,
Pull droopingly, in slanting curve aside,
Their scantly-leav'd, and finely tapering
stems,
Had not yet lost their starry diadems
Caught from the early sobbing of the morn'
(from 'I stood tip-toe upon a little hill')

After the (necessary) emotional inspiration or drive to capture some life experience I travel via different roads to the achievement of a poem.

Sometimes an idea must stay in the mind for many weeks, sometimes years. Sometimes an idea comes quickly to fruition. In the case of Psalm 23, which stemmed from a desire to interpret what I considered to be the best poem known to me, the framework was dictated by the existing poem of David but the interpretation required several months of research.

The much longer poem 'Unknown Woman' was brought to fruition very quickly after a very strong emotional association with the place of her suicide.

Again, the poem 'Vincent' resulted from a wave of the strongest emotional assocation with the life and sufferings of Vincent Van Gogh. Strangely, although I had visited his gallery in Amsterdam earlier, it was on my visit in 1988 that I suddenly felt a compelling urge to write the poem, after first reading the novel of his life. I was literally possessed by a force to complete the poem quickly, and it thus appeared in the Riverside performance. In the main, the manner of verse creation is a wonder to me and I plan very little. It is I feel the wonder of the 'leading-*duende*'.

Returning to the poem 'Unknown Woman', here is an example of the urgency of the first-strike, to capture important ideas:

'Will someone miss me?'
(the cry comes to me).
Deck out the gravestone
With flowers each year

became:

11

'Will someone miss me?'
(the cry comes to me).
Deck out the sad stone —
Bright flowers to see.

Perhaps more graphically:

'A pavement snuffed a life today,
In quiet Egmond aan Zee.
An unknown woman —
Despatched from balcony high —
Without a cry.
She fell from dizzy height today'

became:

'A pavement snuffed a life today,
In so-quiet Egmond aan Zee.
An unknown woman dropped down from
Sea-view concrete balcony high.
Without a cry she fell ... she fell
From dizzy cruel height today.'

An excellent example of the technique of putting down the thought at once, irrespective of clumsiness, is drawn from the poem 'When I Change My Life':

'You felt the pain of the *idiot* me,
But it's now leaving town, it'll never come back.
A weight off my back, and we'll be together,
And happy forever, when I change my life'

became:

'You felt the pain of the *idiot* me,
But it's now leaving town, ne'er to return.
A weight off my back, together we'll be,
Happy forever, when I change my life'.

Having explained, in some detail, my need to feel powerful emotional 'inspiration' before embarking upon a new poem, there only remains my second objective.

This objective, or hurdle which has to be cleared, so to speak, is the achievement of a form of verse that will read well in public. This is a very strongly felt desire and its achievement in practice has caused a very great deal of work.

This, second objective of achieving 'public readability' is not connected with rhyming of verse. The verse may be rhyming or blank, providing 'public readability' is achieved.

The poems in this collection fall into two divisions:-

General poems
Poems of Iberia

They then sub-divide into:

Poems of nature
Poems of historical association
Poems of personal emotions (expressed in a variety of settings)
Poems relating to literature and plays, including religious themes

And so the quest goes on, to write with compelling sharpness at the cliffs of life.

And now the salutation from the Riverside Studios
readings.

'Welcome to our reading, gentles all!
Join us this night in humble hall.
If your imaginations can run free,
A magic carpet flight you'll see.
Fly then! gentles, with our words,
And coaxing music, soulful dance.
When you return to whence you came,
Diff'rent you'll be, for where you've been!

Now players, play your parts,
And stir the hopeful waiting hearts.
Words of love, sorrow and gladness blend,
But give us all a happy end! ... play on!!'

FOOTNOTE ... to
'The Riverside Collection'

The author financed and produced two readings of this collection of poetry at the Riverside Studios Theatre (Hammersmith, London) on November 6th and November 20th, 1988.

The following team of artistes was engaged for the production:-

Actors
Paul Tyreman

Actresses
Lucy Capito
Jane McKell ... (director — November 6th)
Claire Storey
Dawn Taylor ... (director — November 20th)
Abigail Zealey

Musicians/Composers
Paul Kellet (cello)
Richard Storry (classical guitar)

Dancer/Choreographer
Annie Corbier

Lighting/Sound
Lucy Capito
Gambi Bowker
Claire Storey
Abigail Zealey

UNKNOWN WOMAN

On a visit to Holland in June 1985, I stayed at a block of flats by the beach at Egmond aan Zee.

On leaving the flats one day with a friend, I was pointed to a mark on the pavement and told that an unknown woman had fallen to her death there yesterday.

The newspaper report only stated that a well-dressed unknown woman of around forty years had thrown herself down.

I was strongly moved to leave a remembrance of her and show that someone cared. I also had a mental picture of her spirit flying free.

UNKNOWN WOMAN

1.

A pavement snuffed a life today,
In so-quiet Egmond aan Zee.
An unknown woman dropped down from
Sea-view concrete balcony high.
Without a cry she fell ... she fell
From dizzy cruel height today.

2.

Dutch town of Egmond aan Zee,
Balcony with view o'er sea.
Her frail life came to an end ...
And it saddened, saddened me.
Unknown soul, what did she leave?
(just a mark on pavement hard?)
Hustled away from sight, shock
Space quick-filled by flow of life.

3.

Small pebble on pool so smooth,
(quiet de Vassey's Boulevard).
Pretty Egmond aan Zee, in
Holland's flat but pleasant land.
Who would come to see her now?
Would someone heed the call? or
Would her crumpled body lie
All alone in dim cold room?

4.

Did you see her youthful ways?
(skipped away her girlhood days,
graceful dancing earned much praise) —
Ran through tulip fields and played.

5.

Higher and higher —
Her spirit flies free.
High over coastline —
Of Egmond aan Zee.
Wind in her hair sends
It streaming behind.
Outstretched her arms to
A life much more kind.
Gone now the pain of
The constant rebukes,
Gone now the tears and
The unfriendly looks.
It wasn't her fault,
And not perhaps theirs?
She just didn't fit
Life's carpetted stairs.
Fainter and fainter —
Her happy song sounds,
(no-one will miss her
not being around).
I walked quite close to
That dread spot today.
A pavement quite clean —
All trace washed away.

6.

Someone *will* miss her,
(I cry to the sky).
We'll leave her a stone
— not answer the 'why?'
'To woman unknown,
Cut down in her prime.
We will remember
Each year at this time'.

7.

A whispering wind
Moves trees to and fro.
Flick'ring leaf shadows
On mournful grey stone.
Flickering words for
A life like moth's wings.
Too fragile a soul —
To even console.

8.

We sailed out to sea
From warm cosy land.
My mind dwelt ashore
In dim leafy bower.
'Will someone miss me?'
(a cry o'er the sea).
Someone *does* miss her
(its easy to see).
'Will someone miss me?'
(the cry comes to me).
Deck out the sad stone —
Bright flowers to see.

9.

Oh! wispy-white clouds
'gainst china-blue skies.
Constant sea breezes
Soft-carry her sighs.

10.

Good gentle people
Of Egmond aan Zee.
Please place some flowers
In quiet place for me.

11.

Arrow speeds towards the eye-line,
Takes life-full warmth from tableau spent.
First warning chill of out-run day,
Perhaps a warning note to hear?
Darkness sits stark upon the deep.
Warning note in seaman's minds,
And tilting boats head quickly home.
Now she's lost o'er distant eye-line.
Is it the whistling wind I hear?
Is it happy girlish laughter
Heard long ago in tulip fields?

   ... 'Will someone miss me?'

TUBE

Impressions of a journey from Paddington to Westminster
— on the London Underground in 1977. (the poem was
re-structured in July 1988)

It concerns the feelings of a visitor, not used to life
'below ground'. The Underground system seems a little
menacing and the silent stares of the people unfriendly.

There is a strong feeling of mechanical efficiency and
pressure on the individual, and a great desire to return to
the fresh air and open skies above.

The visitor is welcomed by 'Big Ben' on his return to the
London streets. Perhaps 'Big Ben' feels that the visitor
will soon overcome his first revulsion and adjust to the
Great City — which may offer many pleasant
experiences??

TUBE

In underground, reverberating tube —
Swaying, intruding, whirring, warbling thing.
Quick, fleet-patches of daylight punctuate
Enshrouding darkness with dark-light flashes.

Ringing bells and roar at Notting Hill Gate:
Interloping daylight struggles in through roof
And wall invites — 'to where the flavour is' —
Men sit by fire in blue-hilled, parched-grass scene.

Squeeze and squeal of hard brakes, and floor
vibrates,
All-tingling toes and High Street, Kensington.
On through daylight, people stand — trees — then
dark,
And glimpses of creeper-like cabled walls.

Long, snaking and snarling squeaking coaches,
Dancing spheres on spiral springs await hands.
Dancing to-and-fro so very oddly —
One pair in unison and then another.

People wait in silent resignation —
Except for two Aussie tourists loud.
Passive blonde in green zip-coat stares forward,
Her tatty handbag tells of budget harsh?

Sloane Square's daylight comes into view, then
darkness,
Train flashes by — quick blurr of lighted tubes.
'Down-under' couple study warren guide —
Out at Victoria with packs of maps.

I hadn't noticed change of neighbour here,
So-elegant young girl had joined us where?
White raincoat, maroon nails and watchstrap
matched,
Loose-combed hair, black trousers, fresh un-made
face.

Scarcely left school I guessed, and yet she seemed
Already part of lighted-warren life.
Reading 'The Times' with intelligent stare —
Had she ever asked if she should be there?

High-sounding destination reached at last,
My being craves for daylight and fresh air.
A garish platform, like most others seen,
But 'Westminster' has magic herald ring.

Rush, rush, hurry for the stairs and wide-sky!
Return to breezy river's air above.
Mother of Parliaments' high clock tower
Tells me the time and winks at me as well!

AGNESS'S LAMENT

This poem was inspired by the inscription on a gravestone in a Parish Church in Chorley, Lancashire. Four children from one family died over the six year period 1826/1832.

Their mother was Agness. The first child, named Benji, was 23 months at death, the twins (Benji and Otty), died at only 25 weeks. The eldest daughter, Jane, died three weeks after them (she was age 12).

Just how did Agness feel? How could she bear it? The poet must try to 'tune in' to emotions triggered by events of a type not personally experienced.

AGNESS'S LAMENT

Oh! Benji, darling Benji, sweetest love!
I held you in my loving arms, so snug.
And planned the Summer years that lay ahead,
When you would run and jump and whoop with
glee.

Cursed cruel fate that wrenched you from me,
Snatched you from your mother's tender caring.
Scarce two years I'd known and loved you, Benji,
Oh! Benji, darling Benji, sweetest lamb!

Eighteen-thirty-two, and six years later,
My precious twins died, scarcely six months old.
After you, I'd named one, sweet sweet Benji!
And dearest Otty was our other joy.

But Jane was such a wonderous comfort now,
Just twelve years old and such a lovely girl —
Then *she* was taken, scarcely three weeks on —
It left me stunned and weakened, on my knees.

Benji and my other Benji!
And Otty and my darling Jane!
Now I think I never bore them,
And only in my dreams gave suck.

Blow, blow our wintry winds o'er hilltops bleak,
Rain icy rain o'er countless winters cold.
Quick, oh quick! to wipe a grave's inscription,
From the sight of men and poets' eyes.

Benji and my other Benji!
Dear Otty and my darling Jane!
Now I think I only dreamt them,
Perhaps just dolls of childhood days?

WALKING IN THE WOODS

This is a poem for romantics.

An old theme — the comparison of the loved one to aspects of nature.

A wooded place is chosen in this case.

The lover suffers temporary separation and walks in the wood (where they have often walked together), and sees the lover through the 'minds-eye'

— feeling that the surrounding trees are as the lover's arms?

WALKING IN THE WOODS
(on a February day in 1980)

I walked amongst the trees today love,
Looked up to tapering spires 'gainst sky.
I walked amongst the lichens and the ferns,
And felt the mosses and the evergreens.

I walked, long, and meandered in the glades,
But thought and thought of you, love.
Each time I paused to look and ponder,
I saw you standing there and smiling.

As leaves and branches brushed my cheek,
I felt your hand was there instead.
The gentle breeze that swayed the leaves,
Was as your gentle kiss upon my face.

My hand slid gently over sapling smooth,
And felt the smoothness of your cheek.
I passed my hand across your brow,
And held you to me once again.

I walked and walked amongst the trees,
And asked their peace to fill me.
And then I saw you walking there,
And followed you 'till lost to sight.

But now a sadness comes upon me,
And solace I must find amongst the trees.
Amongst the saplings and the moss I'll kneel,
And press my hands in friendly ground.

Spirit of the woods embrace me,
Friendly sprites console my saddened heart.
Curious creatures from the dingle-dells!
Peace you'll bring through twilight songs.

A COTTAGE IN THE LOIRE

The River Cher in France joins the River Loire close to the
Château Villandry in the lower reaches of the Loire
Valley.

On a hill above the Château is a cluster of old farm
buildings known as 'La Taillandière' (which appears to
mean a place where farm implements used to be made or
sharpened).

The days that Summer were sunny and hot, the
evenings warm and the nights were punctuated by
thunderstorms, and fireballs in the sky. The poem was
written at a table in the garden, surrounded by the hum
of country life.

A COTTAGE IN THE LOIRE
(1982)

* First prize at Chorley Arts Festival

Above the winding Cher that joins the Loire,
Close to the graceful Château Villandry:
'La Taillandière' above the river sits,
Cooled by breezes, nestled in the fields.

Buzz and hum of country life about me,
Small green spider hangs beneath my table.
Fat sheep bleat in morning's misty pastures,
Cocks crow quietly over distant fields.

An old, old dog ambles by the cottage,
Remembers days when life was full of Spring.
A cottage old and full of history,
Steeped in the Val de Loire and all its peace.

Brown-golden winged butterfly fast-flits by,
And white ones too, in frantic chase through trees.
Sharp birds scoop and swoop o'er roofs and tree
tops,
And dip from corner tree to field close by.

Night brings another world of Loire delights,
The stillness brings a peace to hearts in tune:
But there's a symphony of crickets' calls,
And thunder claps and fireballs pierce the night.

Such memories of Val de Loire will last,
And with them thoughts of friendly folk, our hosts.
Dear Madame Hausser's sunny Auvergne smile,
Her husband's Provence-humour warms the heart.

..... Au Revoir! chers amis, Au Revoir!

HAVEN

This poem was roughed out whilst sitting in the Duke of Argyll public house, Brewer Street, Soho, London, on August 29, 1977, at 6pm

This pub had such a richly 'vulgar' decor, with such a wide range of colour and furnishings and various 'bizarre' accessories that the poem must be considered the most difficult that I have attempted; in fact, I abandoned it for eleven years!

The problem was to ensure that it 'read well' in public, and I resurrected it in July 1988, after walking past the pub again (when it was closed).

Incidentally, I thought that the interior was quite beautiful and strangely restful. I have recently visited the Duke of Argyll (August 1988) and was dismayed to find that the whole appearance has been changed.

I can only say that, in my opinion, it is for the worst, and I feel very happy to have preserved in verse the memory of better days.

33

HAVEN

The mists of day's activities still swirl —
O'erflowing to me from warm Summer air,
Snuggled in peaceful, haven paradise —
Still feeling the heart beat of London Town.

Red carpet with swirls and red covered seats,
Frown up at the ceiling, dimmed purple-and white.
Matched by warm-embossed wallpaper floral —
Upholstered blue bench seats cling to the walls.

So-neat carved rails of room-spacers tasteful,
Reflected in wall mirrors, oval and high.
Pictures and pretty plates hang on the walls,
Willow scenes ancient and roses so pink.

Bar top festooned with well-potted green ferns,
Aspidistra in red-necked, odd flowered vase.
Bar front is lined with warm-green light boxes,
Heads and shoulders of womens' silhouettes.

City-suited men stand engrossed, beneath
Two slow-turning fans hung o'er their heads.
Soft music plays — 'those were the days my friends!'
Lively, straight-haired blonde talks with men at bar.

American lovers sit by window —
Pared-down aching girl ogles bearded swain!
Stage-face chokered woman sits with man,
And woman-in-green sits and sips alone.

Haven paradise lies in limbo state,
Whilst one quick-life-pulse gives way to other.
Day's long exhausting business cycle ends
And now night's restful therapy begins!

34

MORNING LIGHT

I have long felt the wonder of each day unfolding — and particularly the growing light.

A new day, not promised, becomes a reality.

The poem tries to relate each new day to the possibilities offered to us — and the poem struggles in an effort to express intense feelings through 'mere words'.

In the final verse, a desperate compression of words takes place.

MORNING LIGHT
(1978)

New light slow-stirs in lightening greyness,
Softly stealing, slow revealing new light.
Light that chases, dispels dark and shadows,
Soft corner-searching, quick-darting sharp light.

Welcome to the light that wakens bird life,
That brings fresh hopeful, lungful morning air.
Enriching, warming balmy Summer air,
Cutting, biting, sharp-toning wintry air.

Nature awakens to the calling light,
And sets about her busy new-light chores.
Man awakens to sense of light on mind,
Tries to see purpose in the lighted day.

Promise of continued life in soft light,
A further chance to shine out as the light?
Another span of wakening-hope time,
Fulfilled hope of day, further day of hope.

Life extended, can it be expanded?
A day not promised bursts upon a soul.
Can morning light bring newly-lighted mind,
Dispel prejudice, bigotry and cant?

Oh, God! I'm hopeful for the lightful day,
Sweet Jesus! grateful for the lightful way.
Longing for light through sleep's uncharted seas,
Smiling at the sweet new-light haven, free.

Oh! spirit warmed by light of fanning day,
Enlightening, wakening, spreading light.
Life full of hope, out-reaching hopeful life,
Lightful, out-reaching lighted lifeful hope.

COUNTRY RETREAT

A poem for lovers of the English countryside, and for romantics.

The subject is the special attraction of the English thatched cottage and its rich gardens.

The poem is really about drawing aside from the high-activity and tension of modern life.

It is about sharing such peace with someone else.

COUNTRY RETREAT
(December 1977) Published in 'Alderley Focus'

A quiet, withdrawn Elysium bower,
So neat-thatched tree-snuggled tiny cottage.
A time-stands-still and heart's beat warming place,
Standing apart, quietly, from tortured throng.

Creaking friendly gate leads to well-trod path,
All-lined with well-established cared-for shrubs.
Heavenly-blue Lithospermum lies snug,
Pink-sphered Pernettya Mucronata pouts.

Sheltered close-in by soft warm ivy walls,
Rich, varied herbs speak out for slower days.
Yellow sparkling Chervil, so-green Parsley,
Blue Balm and Basil, golden flowering Dill.

Magic carpet, elegant purple Thyme,
Pouting, flouncing Marjoram's purply-pink
Matches that of browny-leafed Sage's flowers.
Old world simple elegance of Savoury

The rest of luscious garden-feast indeed,
For those who would imbibe the heady wine.
So-gay Petunia, blue Myosotis,
So-dainty blue Lobelia, Crocus bright.

Creaking floors and cool and shady indoors
Comfort and rest enough in fittings sparse.
Cosy and ancient bedchamber warming,
Soft and inviting, sinking quilted bed.

And so, my love, the jealous world outside,
Can have no place with us in this abode.
To draw aside, e'en for so brief a time,
Is nectar sweet for body, soul and mind.

Embrace tender of slender arms and wrists,
Magical curves of back and slender waist.
Softness in softness, quilted paradise,
Ambrosia nestling, love's sweet embrace.

Raindrops fall gently on casement windows,
Rivulets we trace, faces pressed to glass.
Life force expended, the ancient warming,
New strength gathered from trysting place so quiet.

PORTRAIT OF A BOY

This poem was inspired by a painting carrying this title in
the Tate Gallery, London (I understand that it is at
present on loan to the USSR). The painter was Jacob Van
Oost I, of the Flemish School: 1601/1671. I came across
this painting by surprise in a corner of the gallery and
was captivated. It is a head-and-shoulders portrait of a
young boy. I was 'rivetted to the spot' for twenty minutes
and wondered just who this boy was, and how anyone
could portray (on a flat canvas) — such depth of feeling.
The poem tries to describe the painting and identify the
boy. Surely it is the painter's son??

PORTRAIT OF A BOY

I almost walked past you, dear child,
In gallery-corner shaded.
A chance look o'er shoulder caught you,
Nestling in that small, awkward place.
It seemed as though your portrait quiet,
Was added as an afterthought.

But that quick chance-look transfixed me —
I was beguiled from all around.
By what strange artist's sourcery,
Did humble paints and canvas join?
To cause such sweet-light effusion,
To radiate from background dark?

The light! Yes, it was the magic light,
That glowed from hopeful, open face.
Open, clear-eyed receptiveness,
A living, reaching hopeful look.
Wizardry of pigmentation,
Soft spread of light on youthful skin.

The brush has exquisitely caught,
unlimited . . . . expectancy.
Mind free of prejudice and cant —
No canker of the mind or lie.
Soft light's aura from master's wand,
Draws a sigh from spirit striving.

Striving to give some expression,
To those who have not gazed on you —
Sweet, gentle, clear-eyed wistful youth,
I'd draw my readers close to you.
Straight look, and poise, his father's gift?
His mother's gentle spirit shines?

Surely, it is the artist's son?
Or one so close to magic hand,
And guiding heart, that draws from him —
Creative cloudburst waterfall.
Inner soul-light of reaching youth,
Pours from the canvas to my soul.

MAN

This poem was written in Portugal at a time of great mental turbulence which led to consideration of the 'state of man'.

Written in a burst of anger, in about one hour, the poem was subsequently condensed to its present form, and offers a philosophical statement which might find common ground with many men??

MAN
(Portugal — April 1983)

What motivates you, sorry one?
To take the thorny complex path you run?
You cannot understand the driving force,
But it will surely set your stormy course.

Sorrow on sorrow hardly balance joys,
Much of your loves are only childish toys.
Your upright stiffnecked arrogance and pride,
May be a mask to hide what is inside.

Is this your destiny, oh! fickle man?
Raise hope on hope, and never give a damn?
Yet in the act of seeming not to care,
Your conscience strikes to catch you unaware.

Some say that from desire you oft should flee,
Avoiding disappointments, can you see?
And yet the lure of pleasure drives you on,
But oft-time transient happiness is gone.

To act the play of life you'll need a script,
To set which way the scales for you'll be tipped.
Who is it writes the script and hires the cast?
The playwright is a shadow from your past?

Before your birth the mould is partly formed,
Through early years your personal wishes scorned.
Then cast into the turbulent sea of life,
You seek quiet havens from the tears and strife.

45

Man does not pause and ruminate too long,
Hard-driven by relentless force he's strong.
Yet in his strength his sickening weakness lies,
He does not know what lies behind his eyes.

A conceited hand-down from God knows where?
Long wrestling with yourself, how will you fare?
A fight unto the death it is indeed —
Pointless for man to cry out to be freed.

Freedom from what? oh, man! one may well ask,
Perplexing questions put his mind to task.
Freedom from selfish drives it may well be,
Or merely from life's burdens to be free.

******

Mourn not too long for desperate wistful man,
He takes his pleasure where and when he can.
Lasting pleasure will rarely come his way,
His only lasting rest may be in clay?

THE SHEPHERD'S (COVENANT) PSALM — Psalm 23

I was thinking some time ago about what could be the best poem in the World (known to me). After much thought, I decided on Psalm 23.

Of course, it all depends on what we mean by 'best'. I took a rather restricted definition of poetry for this purpose: that is, poetry as a form of personal experience and feeling at the interface with life and the many and complex problems of living and 'justifying one's existence', or place in the 'fabric of life'.

It is clear that, in common with all literature appearing in translation, much can be hidden and lost in the process of translation.

Fortunately, the King James version does not lack poetic force and beauty, but it is necessary to read quite widely across the Bible text and also research the Hebrew to really get to grips with what David was expressing here.

I wish to express my appreciation for the help given by Rabbi M.S. Ginsbury, Minister of the Prestwich Hebrew Congregation (Manchester), in the supply of translations from the Hebrew language.

THE SHEPHERD'S (COVENANT) PSALM

In the King James Version

The Lord is my shepherd; I shall not want.
He maketh me to lie down in green pastures: He
leadeth me beside the still waters.
He restoreth my soul: He leadeth me in the paths of
righteousness for His name's sake.
Yea, though I walk through the valley of the shadow
of death, I will fear no evil: for Thou art with me;
Thy rod and Thy staff they comfort me.
Thou preparest a table before me in the presence of
mine enemies: Thou anointest my head with oil; my
cup runneth over.
Surely goodness and mercy shall follow me all the
days of my life:
and I will dwell in the house of the Lord for ever.

(A Psalm of David: 'David's confidence in the Grace
of God')

A poetic interpretation (January 1987)

High shepherd of the wand'ring flock sees me,
Jehovah-Jireh gently leads a lamb.
By whisp'ring streams where rest is surely found,
In pastures heady-green He sets me down.

(I'd longed for wings of dove to fly away).

Oh! His salvation's joy He will renew,
In joyful song He gives me back my life.
In every pathway safe He guides my feet,
He calls me to be back at home with Him.

(In His mountain I will learn His ways).

The Lord, my Lord, he shepherds me,
His rod and staff will comfort me.
Oh! erring lamb, so choked with grief and fear,
Will freely breathe, the heart is given air.

Out from the desert's blistering sand,
Its clefted ground, deep-dark ravines.
Their counter-glare that blinds the eyes,
To beasts of prey that have their lairs.

No evil end I fear, though close to death,
(Though sitting in death's shadow, light springs up).
He covers me, a wall of fire about,
As mountains round Jerusalem, His care
Forever round about my life will stand.

A fugitive, I fled across the dunes,
Conscience and sin relentless on my track.
My life a wilderness of stark contrasts,
And I am hunted down to death, Unless ...

Oh! blissful joy of Shepherd's Tent!
Brown and black lumps are desert homes.
As 'Guest of God' I'm there received,
There I'll recline and eat in peace.

Safe haven of this Shepherd's tent I'll find,
Not there as Sisera in *Jael's* tent.
(Jael of Kenite Heber drove her nail),
But no such deadly fate will come to *me*.

My enemies and mockers draw away,
A table He has set for me this day.
The oil of joy upon my head o'erflows,
And conquers ashes of the contrite soul.

(Righteous reproof shall never break my head).

In all the days that are to come to me,
Upon my heels His mercy follows on.
With lasting mercy He will gather up,
All those who fall and stumble by the way.

(His goodness stirs repentance, erring lamb).

A doorkeeper in His great house, I'd be,
Than dwell in tents of those of wicked hearts.
I'd dwell in halls wherein His honour dwells,
— there'll be no end to my so-humble start.

The painful rack of my time-destined frame,
The clouds of sadness round my troubled mind.
Rejection by my friends I can survive,
The valley of the final darkness I'll not fear.

(But please, dear Shepherd, not a heart disloyal).

I need much more than precious guidance Lord,
In truth, an erring little lamb needs grace.
What might just be a song so fair, becomes
.... an indestructible experience.

LETTER TO A FAR OFF PLACE

This poem is based upon a painting entitled 'Lady Writing a Letter' by Gerard Ter Borch (1613/1681), in the Mauritshuis, The Hague.

I wondered to whom she was writing? I imagined a husband in the East Indies, or some such place. A long-absent husband? It was common enough in those days.

All she wants is to enjoy a normal family life, with her husband and children. Although gentle and retiring by nature, she finds it difficult to restrain her anger at the separation.

LETTER TO A FAR OFF PLACE

(Holland August 1984)

1.

I write dear Charles with heart so full,
And oh! my love, I've lots to tell.
My pen is slow to scratch its way,
The ink runs dry so quick today.

2.

These Summer days seem very long,
I sit alone and sew a lot.
Well-meaning folk can tiresome be,
'Is it a *year* since he went to sea?'

3.

'Is it a year?' I hear them say,
I count *every day* you've been away.
The Winter days dragged their feet,
Muffled hoofbeats in snow-lined streets.

4.

I see you in the East Indies sun,
Thro' mind's eye, my dearest loved one.
Do not despair that we childless be,
In time we'll have a family.

5.

Your mother called the other day,
(We've talked more since you went away).
She worries that you sail the seas,
Oh! do take care each day Charles, *please*!

6.

My room is dark this late evening,
The flickering candles cast moths' wings'
Shadows across the bedroom wall,
I soon must answer dear sleep's call.

7.

Yes! come dear sleep and cosy dreams,
I sit by you near mountain stream.
And look out o'er the azure sea,
By lands that took you far from me.

8.

Caroline talked of you today,
Her lovely twins were born in May.
You know we're friends from childhood days,
Her twin girls have quite different ways.

9.

And now I knit and sew again,
'Tween wistful looks through window pane.
But this time for *our* needs my dear,
We'll use them soon, I have no fear.

10.

If you could see me seated here,
In pool of flickering candle light.
You'd see I wear your favourite blouse,
And earings on blue ribbons hung.

11.

My dearest husband, still a year?,
Before I hold you close, my dear.
In church I pray for you each day,
And hail the winds to speed your way.

12.

Your letter came and things you need,
Are on the seas to you — gods' speed!
I wish to God that it was me,
Not things, that wing their way to thee!

WHEN I CHANGE MY LIFE

The first six verses are based on the song of the same title on the Chrissie Hynde album 'GET CLOSE' (1986). The music is sad but there might be some hope for this relationship???

I imagined a woman who is a hopeless alcoholic or drug addict (or both) — and her partner could stand no more of it?

I'm afraid the relationship is finished — or so I think — and so I've written it.

The author was very strongly moved by the vocal interpretation of the verse by Chrissie Hynde.

WHEN I CHANGE MY LIFE
(1987)

I'll change the path my life will take, I WILL,
The slate of my past shameful deeds wiped clean.
Taut memories of past disgrace subdued,
My path I'll really change, I WILL, I WILL.

Oh! I know you'll forget, you'll forgive me,
Really come back to my arms, share my life.
You'll tell me you love me, clasp my hand tight,
When I change my path, put everything right.

Walking on air in a pathway so new,
The old heartbreak scars fast fading away.
You'll look up to me once more, precious love,
Eager to show me around to your friends.

You'll want me to stay so-close by your side,
Always to be there, when I've changed my life.
No matter where, you'll be proud to declare,
'She belongs by my side', when I change my life.

My heart cries out from the ice-cold abyss,
Cries out aloud for the Sun's warming rays.
The warmth of your love will blank all regrets,
Of the long gnawing pain I brought to your life.

You felt the pain of the IDIOT me,
But it's now leaving town, ne'er to return.
A weight off my back, together we'll be,
Happy forever, when I change my life.

******

Why was it too late? Sun dropped out of sight,
I just didn't see deep-darkening night.
I couldn't have known the wound in your heart,
Would keep us apart, when I changed my life.

Oh! how I hate NOW the idiot me,
How hard of you, Love, to never forgive.
You knew that I worshipped the ground that you
walked,
Yet you trod on my face as I writhed in the dust.

When I change my life it'll be for the NEXT,
My spirit will climb and shake off my past.
Lonely I'll walk but the air will be clear,
Stars shining so bright, when I start my NEW LIFE.

ALEX OUR LOVE

This poem relates to a son, Alex, born to my daughter Ruth, in hospital in Alkmaar town, Holland, Christmas, 1985. Ruth and her husband were living in a small nearby town called Heerhugowaard.

The snow was thick, and the night sky clear and starlit. There was a little lake at the foot of their garden, and a star constellation 'sat on the roof' of Alex's home.

Three of us went to see Alex in hospital and the poetic force of circumstances combined:- the Nativity, the Three Wise men, The Star of Bethlehem. It just had to be a poem!!

Notes on 'ALEX, OUR LOVE'

In general, this poem could only be fully appreciated by those who feel very strongly indeed about life.

The tour de force of the poem is laser-beamed into one verse, verse 6, and it is reinforced by the poetic force of verses 10 and 11. Verse 6 uses rhyme for impact and the word love appears three times directly and twice indirectly. It draws a distinction between the love expressed by the mother and others and there is a strong reference to the Nativity (the Holy Child).

The poetic style is intentionally varied in order to catch the reader emotionally unprepared, and then to drive home the force of the message and successively relieve the intensity of emotional pressure.

The opening three verses set the birthplace scene in innocent descriptive style.

Verses 4 and 5 make a strong comparison with the Nativity and prepare the way for the immense emotional impact of verse 6 — the beaming of love into the young new life.

Whilst the reader has hardly recovered from this shock-wave, a gentle reference is made to the happy state of the child in verses 7 and 8.

Verse 9 sets a 'picture' snow scene, lulling the reader into emotional rest.

Immediately there is an enormous lift of the mind to the stars and the comparison with the Star of Bethlehem (verses 10 and 11).

Two interesting non-rhyming couplets in verse 12 present the baby's sleeping state alongside the onset of dawn against the snow scene.

Verse 13 is a quiet note of security for Alex.

At this stage, the reader has had perhaps more than one emotional assault and an intellectual lift. This exhausted state is encouraged in the next three verses (14,15, and 16), dealing with the journey from Holland and a humorous reference to Alex.

Then, without a division marker, the reader is taken back to the themes of the mystery of the Nativity and the powers of the Universe and finally a simple note of gratitude for this gift of life.

ALEX, OUR LOVE

Heerhugowaard, Holland, December 1985

So-hopeful note of Christmas bells,
From plain Dutch church in quiet place.
Our Alex, gentle love was born,
At Christmas time in Alkmaar town.

Red berries on his garden tree,
See! Jack Frost's icy finger-trace.
Black ducks upon the little lake,
And new babe born this Christmas time.

Cat's paw-prints in the crispy snow,
Icicles twinkle on the door.
Blackbird hops by on white-topped lawn,
And tiny birds shake snow from trees.

******

Came we three as wise men to the crib,
This Christmas time in quiet Dutch town.
We stood in awe and silent wonder,
And gazed upon his peaceful face.

His mother smiled above the pain,
And wondered at the gift of life.
As Mary did so long ago,
(Although in far more humble place).

61

Alex our love, oh! Alex her dove,
Starlight surrounds you, Alex our love.
Sweet light of love, from this day on,
Wrap round your life, beaming upon.

******

Sleeping face and tiny fingers,
Unconscious game of peek-a-boo.
Oh! what yawns and forceful stretching,
Such tiny feet, too small for shoes.

Alex our love, oh! our sweet gentle lamb,
A sleep in our arms, you go far away.
A far away land of sweet baby dreams,
Into your Id's kaleidoscope scenes.

******

Snow has fallen on Dutch landscape,
Moon high above in clear night sky.
Orange street lamp, snowy branches,
Suggests an orange fretwork scene.

I gazed into the clear night sky,
And saw a bowing Pleiades.
The great white plow was tilted low,
It almost touched our white-topped roof.

Oh! Alex, lovely child of life,
The stars have come to wonder, too.
Dear Alex! gentle little lamb,
The ancient stars see something new.

Alex, our love, sleep in your crib,
Crisp snow-scene waits for the dawn's early
light.
Alex, our love, dream out your life,
Snow pictures emerge from out of the night.

Ah! twinkling star of all our lives,
Alex, our pet, our turtle dove.
We'll keep you safe and warm until,
You'll reach and take your place in life.

******

'Prinses Beatrix' draws slow away,
From Hoek Van Holland's snowy shore.
In cosy Holland's snow-capped land,
We leave a sparkling new-life hope.

63

Heading home towards England's shores,
Ploughing through green-heaving seas.
Memories-flood of last few days,
Little Alex tugs our hearts.

New Year's Eve has come upon us,
Alex our love is five days old.
(How he loves his splish-splash bath time!
Opens his eyes in wonderment).

How the hope of man was kindled,
Wise men returned to distant lands.
Taking with them a magic story,
(His mother Mary's precious gift).

Following, we strongly call you,
Great powers of the Universe.
Focus upon out tiny boy-child,
Alex clearly the Force shall feel.

Wise men left the lowly stable,
The mystery of that night held fast.
Now we sing our hallelujah!
For Alexander Marshall Last.

LAURA

The poem is based upon and inspired by Tennessee William's play entitled THE GLASS MENAGERIE.

The idea for the poem was conceived in 1985 and brought to fruition by the Royal Lyceum Theatre Company (Edinburgh) Production, April 1987.

The poem is dedicated to the cast as follows:

Ann Scott-Jones
Emma Dingwall
Andrew Price
Stuart McQuarrie.

Laura is content to spend most of her time in her home, which she shares with her mother and brother, Tom. She has a crippled leg and occupies her time with arranging and re-arranging a large collection of small glass animals on shelves, and listening to gramophone records (the Victrola), with occasional visits to the Zoo.

Her schooldays' hero, Jim, (known affectionately as 'Freckles'), is brought home by her brother, and Jim dances with her, briefly, and kisses her in a rush of careless enthusiasm. He calls himself clumsy (a 'stumblejohn') to have kissed her, and tells her of his impending marriage to Betty, and a boat trip they plan soon.

For a brief moment, Laura had thought that Jim had come into her life for more than a brief encounter.

How will she react?

LAURA

Come to my world of tiny glass creatures,
Touch them and stroke them and move them
around.
Come, share my world of brittle glass creatures,
See! how they shimmer and twinkle with light.

Oh! Jim, how much I admired you at school,
How lovely your voice as you sang in the shows.
HOW UGLY THE BRACE ON MY LEG as I clumped
To my place in the class, the focus of all.

'Blue Roses' you called me, dear Jim I remember,
I longed for your autograph, really I did.
You ask if I liked you — I LIKED you!
MY HEART MISSED A BEAT AT THE SOUND OF
YOUR VOICE.

The animals take up so much of my time,
Here! take the oldest, its nearly thirteen!
Well, he's my favourite, the Unicorn,
The light throws his shadow long to the wall.

Oh! Jim, don't ask such darned awkward questions,
I dropped out of school and college an' all.
I had indigestion from work at the College,
My animals take up so much of my time!

Hold him so gently, the little glass creature,
So fragile he'll break at more than a breath!
He stays on the shelf with a number of horses,
No need to worry, they get along well!

A second effusion of light when I saw you,
Come into my home, dear Jim, this good night.
'A quiet type of girl, somewhat old-fashioned',
That's what you said, Jim — I HOPE IT'S ALRIGHT?

Don't worry, dear Jim, you've broken my favourite,
It's maybe a blessing for him in disguise.
Glass breaks so easily, I know, dear Freckles,
Breaks no matter how careful you are.

Oh! Jim, did we dance tonight to the Waltz tune?
Did you hold me quite close as I stumbled around?
'A little bit higher — right! now don't you tighten'
'I'm afraid you can't budge me' — but goodness you
did!

Oh! little Unicorn, without your tiny horn,
No tragedy, Freckles, so easily they break.
Perhaps now he'll feel a great deal less freakish,
And feel more at home with the horses I'm sure!

Oh! mother, you married a telephone man,
Gallantly smiling at us from the wall!
Telephone man, fell in love with long distance,
Oh! father you travelled — I never knew where.

I play the Victrola and watch my glass creatures,
Play the Victrola and watch the parades.
I've been to the Zoo, seen the beautiful penguins!
The hot humid glass-house with tropical flowers.

Oh! Jim, you called me an old-fashoined girl,
My shyness eclipsed by the wonder around.
'Loosen th' backbone! that's a lot better',
You moved me around in a heavenly Waltz.

You said I was different from anyone else,
My shyness — discovered dissolved in your warmth.
YOU SAID I WAS SPECIAL - blue roses to weeds!
YOU KISSED ME JUST ONCE AND LIFTED MY
LIFE.

I opened my hand, it contained the glass creature,
NO LONGER SO DIFFERENT, NOW I'D BEEN
KISSED?
Why were you a 'stumble-john', just to have kissed
me?
Why talk of your Betty and a moonlit boat trip?

If being in love's made you all bright and new,
Dear Freckles, how clumsy you'd been before that!
Open your hand, here! take the glass creature,
Yes, you must take it, A SAD SOUVENIR.

I've returned to my SAFE WORLD of tiny glass
creatures,
And phonograph records I've played many times.
I'll look out on the street and its noisy processions,
I'll visit the Zoo and the penguins again!

******

Tom's Postscript (Laura's brother)

'I went far away to strange distant places,
Laura, dear Laura, I cannot forget you.
You see, dear, the world's NOW lit up by lightning,
So blow out your candles — oh! please set me free!'

******

Translucent glass creatures sparkle with light,
Glitter and twinkle on LIFE'S CAROUSEL.
I'll reach out to touch the line of smart penguins,
And return to the glass-house of tropical flowers.

VINCENT

The life story, freely adapted in verse, of Vincent Van Gogh, (1853/1890). Born to a Dutch church minister, he is dogged by his father's example and life style, and the 'family philosophy'. Through family contacts, he joins a firm in London and lodges with the Loyer family, (the mother in her late fifties and her daughter aged nineteen). Vincent was then aged twenty. He falls madly in love with the daughter, Eugenie (see later discussion), but is completely rejected by her.

There is a considerable debate as to the facts of Vincent's stay in England. It has even been suggested that he was in love with his landlady, Ursula Loyer, as well as her daughter (Eugenie)! An early undated photograph of Eugenie (with an inset of the man she married in April 1878, Samuel Plowman), compares favourably in facial structure with a photograph taken much later at her school in Wimbledon, but her quoted age of around forty-six is doubtful and it may have been taken close to her death in 1911 aged fifty-seven.

A published photograph of Ursula Loyer, claimed to date from the early 1850s (when she would be aged around thirty-seven) exhibits a woman more beautiful than her daughter. In face of Eugenie's outright rejection of Vincent's advances, he might well have been thrown towards her mother, although it possibly took the form of attempts to convince her of his evangelical beliefs.

Vincent was in fact drawn to older women. *'Il n'y à point de vielle femme'* (there is no such thing as an old woman). He, for example, felt very close to Mrs Annie Slade-Jones, wife of his employer, the Reverend Thomas Slade-Jones, in London though there was no suggestion of any impropriety.

In his desperate loneliness, he no doubt sought solace in substitutes for his own mother (?). It seems that Vincent became emotionally and psychologically entwined with Ursula and Eugenie. In the poem, I will stick with my original choice of Ursula as his first love. It may be that the object of his passion was Eugenie and she gave him nothing, but Ursula (a feeling and compassionate woman, and probably religious) offered the comfort of deep friendship?

After several periods in England, he finally has to give up any plans to marry Eugenie, and the experience of rejection affects him for the rest of his life. On returning to Europe he falls in love with his cousin Kee (Cornelia Vos), who is married and not available.

Vincent then obtains a position as an evangelist to the miners of the infamous Borinage coalfield in Belgium, where he suffers great hardship and is finally ill. He is dismissed from his position as a minister because of his adoption of a life of poverty. Returning home, he finds Kee free to marry, as she has been widowed. She completely rejects him.

In the Hague he befriends a street girl, Christina, and they live as man and wife for a time. She rejects him finally because he has no money to support them.

Once again at home he continues his true vocation in life (discovered in the Borinage): that is, painting. His brother Theo supports him financially.

Vincent finds friends amongst the peasants and weavers, and Margot falls madly in love with him. His plan to marry her is crushed by her family, and he joins Theo in Paris. He is captivated by the work of the Impressionist group of painters in Paris.

Seeking escape, later, from the City, he takes up residence in Arles, on the Rhone in southern France. He is transformed by the glorious sunshine and varied colours and he paints furiously. He takes in an impoverished Paul Gauguin, but it does not work out (he cuts off part of his own ear in an epileptic fit). Epilepsy takes a grip on Vincent and he has a spell in a mental hospital at St. Remy, but still paints (a painting sells at last, to the wife of the painter Brock).

Theo arranges for him to spend what are to be the last days of his life, at a place named Auvers, near Paris. Epilepsy increases its hold ... and Vincent shoots himself whilst in the fields.

Theo, who has loved and supported Vincent for many years, is heartbroken, and dies six months later, and is buried next to his brother at Auvers. Vincent died in poverty, as he had lived for many years, but left an enormous number of paintings for us to see.

The use of the word 'Pouponne' in the poem is interesting and is based uncertainly on a number of sources. Ursula and Eugenie undoubtedly ran a kindergarten, and one source claims that Eugenie also ran a doll's shop. (Note that the French word for doll is Poupée).

'Poupon' (-onne) refers to a baby, baby-faced (boy) (girl), and a 'Pouponnière' is a day nursery.

One source refers to Eugenie as 'the angel of the little dolls' and another as 'l'ange aux poupons', perhaps best translated as 'little childrens' angel'?

I searched for an extreme expression of newly-discovered love and passion, to describe Vincent's state of mind.

'Pouponne, my angel baby face', seemed fitting

Here is Ursula (or is it Eugenie?) idealistically on a

pedestal of admiration ... an angel caring for the little ones and an object of extreme innocence and vulnerability in Vincent's eyes ... and needing his love and protection.

Vincent had always craved to live in the warmth of traditional family love (he had been very moved to see this in the Vos family ... Kee, her husband and their eight-year old son, Johannes).

Vincent is quoted as saying ... 'I never saw nor dreamt of anything like the love between her (Eugenie) and her mother'. Vincent would naturally have been doubly and very powerfully drawn towards this source of warmth.

The whole truth may never be known about Vincent's stay in England. It may be that some material has been destroyed.

Vincent's mother seemed to disapprove strongly of the Loyer household. She did not think they were a 'normal family', and said there were too many secrets there (!). She wrote to Theo on October 1874, saying that the secrets of the Loyer household were not having a good influence on Vincent. Much was probably locked up in the strange role played by Mrs Loyer.

Vincent's mother was probably overreacting, as she naturally worried about Vincent's life. A letter which is not included in the published letters of Vincent seemingly indicates that Vincent considered Mrs Loyer a 'born-again Christian' and Vincent was deadly-serious about his religion at this point in his life.

VINCENT

(September 1988)

His period in England ...

URSULA

Oh! England and your scattered skies,
My scattered hopes I'll leave behind.
(Ursula Loyer, little dove,
I threw myself at you in love).
Pouponne, my angel baby face,
You drew me into life itself,
Yet offered nothing to my soul.

The torment of your pouting lips,
Had forced from me an urgent kiss.
'Red-headed fool!' — your searing words
Crushed all my finest, tender hopes.

An outcast from your happy home,
I fled to Breda and my father's talk.
That I should follow in his path,
Minister'ng to souls of men? —
When my own soul was torn in shreds!

Drawn, yet again, to my own precious love
I stood outside her home at Christmas time.
I stood in love's most hopeful happy state —
A door slammed in my face caused cruel pain.

74

Flight once again across the sea,
The months in Dordrecht tortured me.
So once again to England's shores,
To Ramsgate and an unpaid job.
Two dozen boys I had to teach,
But nothing took her face from me.
Long tiring walks to London Town,
For just a glimpse of my dear love.

In rising passion's driving force,
I joined a school in Isleworth.
Teacher-turned country curate then,
I felt a stranger on the Earth.

Drawn once again to my beloved Pouponne,
I saw her married to another man.
Oh! crushing practicality of life,
I saw at last the awful painful truth,
Love-blinded eyes had never seen before.

Oh! Ursula, my first true love, my Pet,
My darling and my gentle turtle dove!
Gone forever, our chance of sweet embrace,
Gone forever, my hopes of balanced life?

Oh! England, never to your white-cliffed shores
Will I return, lest I should glimpse my love.
And so my weeping eyes will ne'er meet hers,
With Ursula cast forever from my mind?

*****

2. INTERLUDE ... and Kee (Cornelia Vos)

Amsterdam seemed very bleak,
(At least it was to my sore smitten heart).
Until I met my cousin Kee.

Hair twixt blonde and red,
And deep blue, smiling eyes.
We walked and talked of Rembrandt's work,
And touched upon the Word of God!

I met her loving husband, Vos,
And sat their son upon my knee.
I felt engulfed by family love,
So needful to my aching soul.

*****

3. THE BORINAGE (coal mining region in South Belgium, near Mons)

Much too easily persuaded?
I went to preach in that sad place.
Black-Egypt's waste-tip hills scowled out,
A trademark of the Borinage.

Smoke-blackened, still thorny hedges,
Seemed crocheted against the snow.
Dead-black trees and choking ash dumps,
Heaps of useless coal squint out.

I had not thought that men could work,
In such a place as Marcasse mine.
I saw the hard Marcasse routine,
Down to the depths at crack of dawn.
Men and young children (boys and girls),
For thirteen hours entombed below.

A bitter Winter took its toll,
And typhoid reared its ugly head.
I moved into an earth-floored hut,
And shared my wealth with those in need
Of simple food and cover warm.
I tore my skin in icy earth,
To scrape rude coal from coal hill cold.

*****

At last, first bright sign of Spring
My sickness now began to ease.
And then the Marcasse monster struck,
Near sixty men and children dead!

*****

Why was the church so critical?
So sure that I should be dismissed?
I'd given all to my 'blackjaws',
The miners of the Borinage.

*****

But now, in all my black surround,
I took to sketching all around.
And this a fire awoke in me,
Here was the path that I should take?

77

Dear Theo came when I was ill,
Dear, caring Theo, brother dear.
Two years away had been too long,
He offered help, to chart my course.

*****

4. *ETTEN* (Vincent returns home to Etten — age 27)

A *widowed* Kee took me quite by surprise,
I opened my creative heart to her.
I had to offer marriage, I just had,
Why did it strike such terror in her soul?

*****

5. *THE HAGUE* (Christina found and lost)

Christina (my Sien) came to my barren life,
Through chance encounter in a coarse wine bar.
A street girl, my Sien, a laundry worker,
Already has to feed five children,
And there's another on the way — not mine.

*****

'Please Sien, do please try to understand,
My new-discovered magic world of oils
Must take our money and the pride of place.
But did you really need to say goodbye? —
You were to all intents my caring wife.'

*****

78

6. THE POTATO EATERS
(returns to his parents' home again)

Now to the blessed peaceful freedom,
To walk the fields where peasants work.
To see the weavers at their looms,
And capture all of Nature's force.

Here now at last I saw, I understood,
That I must work my paints with increased speed.
To capture first impressions of the scene,
In creative energy's quick-sharp bursts.

*****

Margot Begeman, you loved me,
You fell in love with me at sight.
Seemed so right that we should marry.
Your family couldn't stomach me.

*****

Oh! God, how very lonely can one feel?
A peasant family took me to their hearts.
De Groots' potato eaters, my dear friends.
Their daughter, Stien, felt drawn to me.
We walked and talked in innocence.
(the kerkmeester had made her pregnant,
But accusations came my way).

Sadly, I must leave the Brabant,
Theo and Paris beckon me!

*****

79

7. *PARIS* (Vincent discovers the Impressionists — and his life can never be the same)

Paris! all that had gone before,
For me, was wiped as clean as new.
I saw Impressionists at work —
A bolt of lightning crossed my brain.

Henri Toulouse-Lautrec at Rue Fontaine,
Quite close to Degas, don't you know?
Paul Gauguin at Restaurant Bataille,
(I was stunned to see his work).
Blazes of colour in violent contrast,
And scenes all-quiv'ring with pulsating life.
A wild explosion of the golden Sun,
It's heat and intense light pervading all.

Gauguin took me to Georges Seurat,
Brilliant use of dotted light.
Then to the house of Henri Rousseau,
And Emile Zola's friend, Cezanne.

*****

8. *ARLES* (old Roman settlement, on the Rhone)

Oh! God I needed sun, the warming Sun.
It struck me with great force and kindled fire.
And split my senses in a hundred ways,
Lemon and yellow light and harsh-blue skies.

I had to work at frenzied pace,
To make a canvas every day!
Neat-tilled fields and blossomed orchards,
All set against a mountain scene.

80

Good food was difficult to get,
I worked on absinthe and my smokes.
And everything around seemed burnt,
As Summer fast approached it's end.

Canvasses, bright burning yellow,
And drenched all over by the Sun.
Sun-steeped and sunburnt displays,
I tried to give the feel of flowing air.

I crossed the Place Lamartine with our postman,
And saw a rentboard on a yellow house.
With two wide wings and narrow centre court,
And spacious top and ground floor rooms.

A letter came, it bore sad news,
Paul Gauguin poor and sick to death?
A virtual prisoner in Brittany,
I'd free the prisoner, take him in!

*****

VINCENT'S HOUSE AT ARLES (1888)
(two years before his death)

A happy house of golden-yellow light,
Set stark against a bright intense-blue sky.

Oh! Arles, bright-yellow sunny peaceful Arles!
Full of Earth's springtime — (*near my Winter's end*).
Surrounded here at every hand
By friendly colours, tints and hues.

81

GOLD AND YELLOW AND SHADES OF BOTH,
REFLECTED LIGHT OF GOLDEN SUNNY RAYS.
Gnarled trees greens try to balance glare.
Ah! but keep the yellows, brightly shining —
Falling like cooling-waters on a thirsty soul.

Wrestle and fight, struggle with colours mixed,
The fight that must be waged until the end.
A restless, tortured soul still strives for truth,
To reconcile life's light-dark patchwork quilt.

*****

'YES, AS NOW I SENSE THE HASTENING END
STILL FROM MY BRUSH THE BRIGHTNESS
FLOWS'

*****

YELLOW ON YELLOW, GOLD ON GOLD,

BRIGHT YELLOWS BRIGHTLY FRAME THE GOLD.

YELLOW, YELLOW AND YELLOW ACHE THE
EYES,

The Spirit feels continuing surprise!

*****

The Winter passed away, springtime approached,
And still Paul Gauguin did not come to stay.
Then Summer brought the great man to my place,
BUT WHY, OH! WHY MUST HE DESTROY MY
WORK?

Why, dear Paul, did you decide to leave?
I had not meant to threaten you, dear friend.
The open razor was not meant for you,
It took away my ear, in sudden fit.

At least I knew now of my plight,
And fits would come and tear my life apart.
Kind doctor Rey gave me his good advice,
I must go into care at St. Remy.

The hospital, a dark-quiet sombre place,
Monastery of St. Paul de Mausole, an ancient place.
A Roman settlement of long ago,
It seemed a peaceful place for me to rest.

*****

9. *ST. REMY* (at the mental hospital)

The tightening grip of raging fits,
Would be my lot from that time on.
Once more allowed to walk across the fields,
I PAINTED CYPRESSES THAT REACHED THE
SUN!!

I was so pleased at all around,
— And then a seizure in the fields.
GOOD NEWS FROM THEO, MY FIRST SALE!!
'Red Vineyard' to dear Anna Brock

*****

10. *AUVERS*

(one hour from Paris, a move arranged by Theo, to be in the care of Dr. Gachet, an art enthusiast and subsequent unswerving believer in Vincent)

How kind of you, dear caring Theo,
To call me back up North and into care.
To Paris and the calls of my old friends —
Toulouse-Lautrec, Rousseau and Père Tanguy.

*****

In café Ravoux I took a room,
In l'Oise valley's little Auver town.
My grip was weakening now, I fear,
The brush, it slipped and spoiled my art.

I'd worked so hard, you see,
(Prolific output takes it's toll).
My candle now was near burned out,
July would bring my next attack.

But I still tried to work in Summer Sun,
In yellow cornfield by the cemetery.
I painted 'Crows Above a Cornfield' there,
BUT LIFE HAD BECOME IMPOSSIBLE, I FEARED,

*****

THE TRUTH FIRST-DAWNED ON ME AT GOLDEN ARLES

NOW IN MY MIND STOOD STARK IN AWFUL TRUTH.

I'M NOT SURE WHERE I FOUND THE FATAL
GUN,

BUT IN THE FURROWED FIELD IT DID IT'S
WORK.

*****

11. *LAST JOURNEY* (Auvers)

Black horses and a little matching hearse,
Passed slowly down the narrow sunlit road.
And so very slowly climbed the low hill,
Through sweeping yellow cornfield's waving sea.

******

'You did not have to follow me, dear Theo —
So soon, why, — it was only six months on.
You could not stand the grief, I know too well,
So very great a love you'd had for me.

*****

12. *SAINT THEO*

What can be said of such a brother true?
O'er all those years I struggled with my art.
Supported me from his own meagre purse,
Nor did his faith in me once falter,
Through all my desperate searchings for the truth.
From Arles he cared so deeply for my health,
And to the end arranged a caring friend.

85

DID EVER ANYONE DESERVE SUCH LOVE?

I WAS A MAN SO FORTUNATE, I SEE

FOR LOVE AND CARING ARE WITHOUT PRICE,

AND THOSE WHO GIVE THEM, OR RECEIVE,
ARE BLEST.

*****

To those of you who'll judge my life,
I pray that you will see my work.

— AND IF YOU'RE PLEASED, LET THEO HAVE
YOUR PRAISE!!

*****

POSTSCRIPT

Waving golden cornfields in the Summer breeze,
Tall and swaying golden sunflowers beaming.
Vincent and Theo soft-rest together
In shadows 'neath the golden-yellow light.

Rolling sea of yellow, glistening yellows,
And waving gold-on-gold against the sea.
See! yellow on gold, and gold on yellow,
VINCENT HAS MADE IT CLEAR FOR US TO SEE!!

VIEW FROM ALDERLEY EDGE

The only real piece of elevated land in the whole Cheshire plain, Alderley Edge is a rocky height, covered with forest and honeycombed with mine workings. It has a history of wizards, in legend. In fact, there is an inn, on the edge, named 'The Wizard'.

The Edge abounds with peaceful walks through woods and farmland. The view from the cliffs of the Edge is breathtaking and there are two airfields in the near-distance. The flat plain stretches around as far as the eye can see, except for the mountain range to the East, and its highest peak, Kinder Scout, can be seen in the foreground.

The writer was gripped by the thought of the immense volcanic activity that thrust the Edge up from the surrounding plain.

VIEW FROM ALDERLEY EDGE

(Cheshire, on a July day, 1977) — published in
Alderley Focus, April 1978

By cataclysm hurled to dizzy sight,
Unseen, powerful hand, squeezed time-marker tube.
Above fair flat land, running far to sea,
Deep-down, man-marked foreground nibbled green-
swards.

Encompassing-hedged tree-peppered soft swards,
Slow-shuffled by black-and-white chewers of cud.
Far down view seems painted on green backcloth,
But there! to keen sharp eyes, slight movements
seen.

Farm buildings' cluster is split by winding lane,
Curved roofed toy barn high-stacked with Winter
feed.
Gleaming-white brown-roofed house snuggles by
trees,
Up-ranked by stately house's steep-pointed roof.

High-noon shadows lie below dotted trees,
Fingers of shadow claw from wooded hill.
A still picture of softly-varied greens,
White birds hover and drop on foreground field.

Patchwork of cropped and grazed fields yawns away,
Distant airfield gives sight of silver birds.
Toy tractor crawls below, towing cart of blue,
Overseen by lanky pylons, grey and slim.

Faint noise of farm machine and passing train,
Winged bird of man's making cuts still air.
See! low, grey backcloth of fus'ed cloud,
And higher, light-blue pastel sky puffs cloud.

ON LEAVING DENMARK

This poem was written on the ship, on leaving the port of
Esbjerg, in August 1983.

It was our first visit to Denmark, and we had stayed at
a Summer house near Copenhagen, on the south shore of
the Kattegat.

ON LEAVING DENMARK
(Esbjerg, August 1983)

Silently we quit your neat, quiet shores,
Without fuss our high-white ship slips its lines.
Oh! quiet and peaceful gentle land,
We'll not forget your caring hand.

Pleasant, angular folk, with ready wit,
You set a pleasant scene for travellers' eyes.
Land of many islands, sheltered waters,
Ordered fertile farmlands, forests shady.

Old Summer house, close by chilly waters,
Holds fast memories into distant past.
Those, as girls, who ran and laughed and played
there,
Still cling in hope to ghosts of yesteryear.

Soft, warming wind across the Kattegat,
Taking bobbing yachts Easterley to home.
Startling sunset shines across the waters,
It fights and lingers long, 'gainst call of night.

The Summer house calls folk from far and near,
They go for rest, (some take their burdens there).
Some at the start of unclear path of youth,
Experienced travellers seek new ways of truth.

What do we seek — you quiet and gentle land?
Time passes through life's hour-glass like the sand.
Turbulent, troubled lives lived at high pace,
May somehow learn a lesson from this place?

LAMENT

An old theme, of a 'lost love'.

The partner has perhaps listened to untruths and has been influenced to break away? But why would he/she do that without asking if they were lies? And so on ... an attempt to portray the 'tortured mind of love'.

LAMENT
(1980)

Fear not the common spark 'twixt souls
That tread a sympathetic path.
Douse not that friendly light so warm,
For it can bring a balm so sweet.

She has, I fear, to others tuned
And heard unkind and untrue things?
Hurt her I would not, nor could I
Bring ought but pleasure to her soul.

Life's paths which cross one time by chance,
May part and cross, and cross again.
At crossing points the light of hope
Burns brightly and the heart is quick.

Once I held her, briefly, warming,
Gently held her cheek to mine.
Kissed her gently, held her softly,
Precious moments lost in time.

Now it seems the wind so chilling,
Moves across life's barren plain.
Although she'd seemed so very willing
— I'll never hold her close again?

BRIDGET

This poem might be an attempt to describe a meeting between a heterosexual man and a very attractive woman who is 'of the opposite persuasion'.

He is dismayed at the rebuff and lack of sympathetic feelings.

She tells him that she was thrown out of her home by her parents when she was sixteen and, although he feels great sympathy for her, there is no encouragement for him at all.

The poem is an attempt to imagine his feelings in this situation.

BRIDGET

(September 1978)

The million miles that seemed to separate
Two thoughtful people in the stream of life:
Bridged by a miracle? — it's hard to say,
But sure, my spirit soared on eager wings.

For one fast-fleeting spell that felt the force
Of a sweet wish that it would never end.
I took your hand in mine and felt its warmth,
My arm about your waist felt no rebuff.

What's in a brushing kiss upon a cheek —
Half pulled away and hesitantly held?
So much that's warm and intimate it seems,
And we should not be damned to stay apart.

We're told that we should not be drawn, and yet
I felt the warmth of vital life was there.
Quench not that warmth or else resulting cold
May leave a life the poorer, can you see?

Let tender understanding be our guide
To such sweet unexplored delightful shores.
If fate will yet allow we'll meet again,
With further understanding in the heart.

HILARY

A poem which tries to describe a brief-encounter between two people known to the author.

The woman was an actress who at first encouraged her partner but it was soon clear that she was rather immature, unbalanced and self-destructive.

She could only disappoint.

HILARY
(1977)

I hope you'll be a friend 'cos you lift me,
Your kisses are so sweet and they free me.
Can you understand, it's a kind of wonderland?
So let's keep a friendship true — hold my hand.

Your funny little quirks — so beguiling,
No matter if you're just angry or smiling.
Could you be reaching out for something new?
You see, maybe I could be reaching too.

When first we met I wasn't sure to try,
But then, you build a fence so very high.
You've been around I know and that breeds care,
But trust can grow as you the wonder share.

Cheek-to-cheek, such rare tenderness we share,
My hand strokes gently down your silk-soft hair.
We brush each other with kisses tender,
Words needn't pass between us — remember?

With fear I view your self-inflicted pain,
And yet you turn your back on me again.
Don't brush aside a friendly helping hand,
Your attitude I just can't understand.

I hope you'll be a friend — you're a sweety,
I hope your heart accepts — my entreaty.
I hope you'll be my friend — 'cos now it seems
That sweet desire no longer lives in dreams.

GOODBYE (to a spacewalker)

Inspired by a story by Arthur C Clarke, it tries to portray the extreme loneliness and courage of astronauts. Imagine a small crew of astronauts on the first mission to a distant planet. All the crew, except one, have been killed by some virus. In such circumstances, the survivor is instructed to make some transits of the planet, taking photographs, and then return to Earth.

Our survivor, who has waited many years for this, his last chance to reach this planet, and possible fame, decides on a bolder plan. He will descend to the surface on his own and chance a disaster. The poem speaks of mankind's ceaseless quest for knowledge, and tries to involve the reader in the problems (and drama) of space travel. Travel with our spacewalker in your minds, and feel fortunate not to be actually sharing the experience!

A poem to the 'Spirit of Mankind': fasten your seatbelt!!

GOODBYE

(inspired by Arthur C Clarke)
(written 1977. Restructured July 1984 — and again in
July 1986 — and again in December 1988)

Across great yawns of slow-ticking space-time,
How long had passed in *Earth's* measure of time?
Seemed like forever in measure of heartbeats,
Skywalker had lost all sense of his time.

Bright stabbing light rays on dense bright-green
backcloth,
Clouds of deep orange, billowing like foam.
Reverberating, jolting, wild claps of thunder,
Showering iced-plumes from quick-frozen droplets.

A floating, spiralling, oft' bucking free-fall,
A stomach-plucking tense high-ride through space.
Spiralling, wobbling, orange-green blurring —
Through spuming ice-diamonds falling so fast.

Splashing and dashing, lashing rain droplets,
Blurring, obscuring what lies down below.
Wool-like and gaseous, dense clouds of purple,
Reflect and deflect bright sharp-shooting rays.

Slow, dizzying, head-over-heels pitching —
Over-and-under to stabbings of light.
Orange and silver, green blue and purple —
A spinning and giddy carousel ride.

Reeled senses struggle and strive for control,
Eyes try to shut out the needles of light.
Far down below a view of — (what was it?)
Staring-hot cauldron, hot mountains jagged.

Stomach-pitting, a gut-sickening dragging,
Draining of spirit and strength of resolve.
No turning back — predictions precise *there*,
(grotesquely wrong about terrain below).

Faster and faster, flitting bright landscape,
Through green torrid spumes of hot spraying jets.
Swirling steam clouds obscure jagged rock face,
Forced now to land but no safe place is found.

*****

Red dust cloud marks the shattering impact —
Nothing records Earthman's unobserved death.
'Midst glistening wreckage, strange birds' sharp-
beakings
Leave only parched bones to fierce greedy winds.

Searing winds whine across hot-burnt red landscape,
Hot sand rushing, swirling and rattling the
Picked clean-white bones of our deep-space
outreacher.

*****

Others may find this place more inviting??
NOTHING'S MORE CERTAIN THAN MORE MEN
WILL COME.

ON THE LOSS OF A YOUNG CHILD

A young teacher, a colleague of the writer, lost her first child (at the age of four months). The tragedy took place whilst the child slept in the pram in the garden on a very hot Summer's day.

It is thought that the child was too heavily clothed and blanketed, and consequently overheated and suffocated. A terrible tragedy.

The poem tries to take the place of the mother and tries to be encouraging to the 'desolate spirit'.

ON THE LOSS OF A YOUNG CHILD
(1981)

(a four month old's 'cot death')

I'll not rage against the force that took you:
And naught can take the joy I had, from me.

Not to see a solid wall before me,
But the filtering light of life and hope.

Yet rage I must at times until, when spent —
My inner strength will gently speak to him.

And something else will also speak to me —
To raise me from my knees and lift my head.

That voice — the ancient life force, calling —
Speaks hard to me from those who've gone before.

Calls from those who've suffered heartache, too —
And stood up proudly from the parching dust.

Yes — I'll rage and beat my arms about me,
But in the quiet of my soul, draw peace.

HEART CRY

A short poem on a tragic theme. It attempts to portray complete depression.

A person who has reached 'wits end corner'. — or feels that he/she has come to that point.

HEART CRY
(1980)

Like a pack of cards, my hopes — cascading,
Whatever ray of light there was — fading.
What was the radiant beam that offered hope?
A fleeting will-o'-wisp became a joke.

Mischievous joker, act your rotten part,
Pursue your aim to wound the feeling heart.
From the depths of misery hope can rise,
And from burnt ashes build a sweet surprise?

Alas! sweet surprise turns sour at taste,
And jesting joker jostles by in haste.
To douse the ray of hope that tempts a fool,
To think that he's not just the joker's tool.

MOTHER

Notes of amplification would be pointless, here.

Those who had a beautiful relationship with their mothers and suffered such a bereavement will truly understand.

MOTHER

From early years I loved her so —
(There was no need to speak of it).
When times were hard her faith was strong,
And never faltered by the way.

In latter years her wasting frame,
Stood stark against her strength of heart.
I wished I could *my* strength impart,
To see her stand and walk again.

I held her hands in mine that week,
Before her flight from this tired scene.
I knew she knew the end was near,
And yet she gave a word of cheer.

I stood in awe beside the box,
And gaped in disbelief and grief.
Was it a waxen sculpture there? —
(It could not be the life I'd known)?

I KNOW

A poem relating to 'Christian Certainty', and peace.
The poem is one of thematic development. From a 'garden of achievement' (Gethsemane), to a place of spiritual rest and liberation. Then to a lasting joy, and finally to the heavenly destination and continual bliss.

I KNOW
(1959)

(2nd Timothy, Chapter 1: verse 12)
(First Prize, Chorley Arts Festival, Lancs)

I know a garden quiet and still,
Where Satan strove to break His will.
Alone our Saviour anguished there,
To do the Father's will His prayer
— In dark Gethsemane.

I know a place of perfect rest,
A place of calm repose, so blest.
Where distressed souls can draw aside,
From fears and Satan's power to hide
— The place called Calvary.

I know a place of blest retreat,
Where with my Saviour I can meet.
A heart once burdened and in night,
Strong wings of eagle took in flight
— The place, my Saviour's feet.

I know a joy no words can tell,
That springs from out salvation's well.
Of living waters fresh and clear,
Purchased by royal blood so dear.
— The joy in Christ, my Lord.

I know a place in heav'ns above,
For those beneath His banner Love.
Where Sun no longer needs to shine,
Illumined presence, so divine!
— The place called Paradise.

DISILLUSIONMENT

This was a first attempt at surrealism — the title came *after* the poem was written!

Having no idea how to even *start* such a poem, I 'programmed my mind' with the idea and left it for some months.

Suddenly I had the inspiration to write this decidedly odd piece!

It may describe a totally disillusioned (sensitive) person who has not found an accepted place in a puzzling (and menacing) society or environment??

Originally written in 1977, and re-structured in December 1988.

note:

Dictionary definition of 'surrealism':
'a form of art in which an attempt is made to represent and interpret the phenomenon of dreams and similar experiences'

DISILLUSIONMENT

Floating down slowly on cotton-wool clouds,
Sleepy-eyed, half-asleep senses all dulled.
Nearer and nearer to cheese-covered land's
Soft spongy surface and iced-castle high.

Splud! and kerplosh! in the cheese with my shoes,
Struggling and wrestling to stay on my feet.
Iced-castle towers high, on yellow cheese plain,
Unpack the snow shoes and make for its walls.

Cheese footprints trail, twisting and winding,
through
Candy-floss trees and iced-sugar bushes.
Up cold steep hard cheese, rock-candy-strewn slopes,
To toffee-layered drawbridge of iced-castle high.

'Let me in, let me in!' loudly I cry,
A snuffling is heard on the high sweetmeat wall.
Loony-elephants leaning (just hear them crow!) —
Such drooping long trunks and saucer-like eyes.

Whooping cries trumpet from trunks held up high,
Kangaroo goats join the hullabaloo.
A ding-bat platypus zooms overhead —
'Bang the bridge post with your fat silly head!'

Rat-a-tat-tat with my head on the post,
Answering moan from lazy fat bat mole —
'Must say the password (it's 'Dopey' you know)',
'Dopey' it is then, and 'Dopey' I cry.

Drawbridge clumps down on hard frozen toffee,
Skate on my hands over sweet surface smooth —
To giggles of goats and platypus squeals,
Loony-trunks trumpeting, squawking of birds.

Glistening rooms, thick-layered with sugar,
Soft-cheese-floor peppered with marzipan statues.
I flip and I flop with snow shoes so clumsy —
Toffee-lined forehead and blue frozen nose.

Loony elephants bugle in long tidy rows,
In creature-crammed, glistening banqueting hall.
My slithering steps met by loud screeching laughter,
I fall into bottomless meringue-lined pit.

Giddying, spongy, buffeted free-fall,
Weird loony creatures tumble and jostle.
Squeaking, screeching and trumpeting gaily,
All lost forever in pink meringue world.

TECHNICAL NOTE:

Ten four-line blank verses. Six verses follow ten
syllable (iambic pentameter), being verses 1,2,5,6,7
and 10. Verses 4 and 8 follow 10,11,11,10 pattern and
verse 9 follows 12,11,12,11. Verse 3 follows 10,10,10,11

POLITICAL PRISONER

This is a poem inspired by the special fate of this type of prisoner, especially bearing in mind that they are not criminals and are often patriots.

I was burdened by the injustice and loneliness of the prisoner's state, and the lack of hope, coupled with neglect of fundamental needs and rights: and often bad treatment, including torture.

In the midst of the crushing sadness is a note of hope — for others.

POLITICAL PRISONER
(October 1982)

I look around my Kingdom dripping-dank.

There's little of life except a high and oblong slot
To open sky and clouds.

Fifteen long years have dragged me out,
On time's great rack in wasting damp,
Sun's bright tick-tock pendulum
Is abacus of changing sky-slot.
The pain of rotting teeth passed by
(they ignored all my cries for help),

No word of comfort, human voice,
No paper, pen or book in here.
No warming flame or warming food
To break the dead damp chill so drear.
Long years ago I scratched a cross
Upon the cold-cramp, cold-damp wall.

A spider spins industriously.
Busy cockroach slow-fumbles on,
And seems as blind to world as I.

Night shadows fall, (I have no lamp).
The cold bites in and dampness too.

Some day all men will freedom breathe.
But come, for me, death's sweet release!

OBITUARY

It could be a (doubtful?) luxury for a poet to write his/her own obituary? At least, it will be too late to write it 'after the event'! I was surprised at not imagining my spirit to roam around any place where I have worked or played in the UK? — but in Granada and its beautiful Summer Palace gardens of the Generaliffe. And in the Loire Valley of France.

OBITUARY

Mourn not for me when I have gone.
Weep not at my extinguished light.
I lived and loved life to the full,
And did the best with what I had.

My words I've left as markers clear,
For future generations sons.
Read, read my burning words and glow,
And feel the pulse of searching life.

I'll walk the Earth in morning light,
When soft nature's veil lifts gently.
I'll hold the dewdrops in my hands,
And wonder at the dewy webs.

*****

You'll find me in Alhambra's shade,
As evening Sun dips out of sight.
Walk quietly in the Generaliffe,
And you will meet my spirit there.

By its glistening tinkling waters,
I'll stand with fingers in the flow.
Look, look up with me and upwards —
To breathless line of snow-capped peaks.

*****

Tread quietly in the Val de Loire,
By ancient Château Villandry.
For I will wander in its fields,
In Summer twilight times so soft.

*****

In such distant haunts you'll feel me,
Hush! and you may in quietness hear.

*****

Take, take, the cup of life from me,
And, tasting, feel the flowing joy —
(Not for the timid is this draught).

LISBOA BOUND

This poem describes my feelings on an evening flight to Lisbon from Manchester. The departure time from Manchester was well after midnight and it was an eerie flight, poised between starlit sky and white clouds below.

People have varied ways of spending their time on flights. Some sit praying for the destination to be reached safely; some play games; others sleep, whilst others talk or drink away the journey. It was a tumultuous period of my life, and I sat with face pressed to the window, peering out into the gathering night.

I thought of the frailty of mankind when seen from a frail bird in the sky.

LISBOA BOUND

(March 1983)

(Evening flight from Manchester to Lisboa)

Winged bird of fire with starchy metal wings,
Slides high o'er sea of wavy cotton wool.
Against a blue and hazy sky, the Sun
Hangs red and low as dusk invites us on.

Silver wings slope away and touch the Sun,
A dipping fireball sinks and shoots its light.
Oh! silver bird, take me to Lisboa fair,
And as I write the orbe sinks out of sight.

High we soar, o'er mankinds' troubled torment,
Soar now, *my heart*, take up new hopeful course.
I will renew my former firm resolve —
And will not yield my spirit, come what may.

Winding river of blackness splits the clouds,
Inside its walls an Earthly river flows.
Steep cloud bank's tumbling chamfer leads the eye
To blackness of the land so far below.

Four twinkling lights in line ahead appear,
And there! — another five sharp points nearby.
A Spanish town on craggy coast below,
Heralds the final stage as darkness falls.

LISBOA

This is an attempt to express the feelings generated by the beautiful City of Lisbon.

The exquisite natural harbour, the great bridge (Ponte Salazar), The river (Rio Tejo), the great castle (Castelo de São Jorge), and the great, inspiring statue of Christ the King (Cristo-Rei), standing over the town with outstretched arms. The poem attempts to take all this in, and feels the ancient history of the place.

LISBOA
(March 1983)

Serene haven of Phoenician naming,
Lisboa on seven low hills sits proud.
The ancient Rio Tejo spills its life
Into the shimmering-gold Sea of Straw.

Conquered by Greek and Carthaginian,
And then again by great and mighty Rome.
Barbarian Visigoths followed on,
And, last of all, the Arab Moorish kings.

Ten tall towers of Castelo de Sao Jorge,
Securely built by Visigoths and Moors,
Look South o'er Tagus estuary wide,
To outstretched arms of awesome Cristo-Rei.

Torre de Belém sits on Northern Bank,
Reminder to all of adventurous times.
Vasco da Gama sailed from here, across
New World's horizon then obscured from sight.

Ponte Salazar stands astride the Tejo,
Two pylons deep-sunk into basalt rock.
A dizzying ride across its steely span,
Taut cables string this instrument of man.

Au Revoir, dear ancient Lissabona,
I left you but there's still so much to see.
Pont Salazar's taut steel back supports me,
To left the sidelong glance of Cristo-Rei.

FADO SINGER

An experience in the Sr. Vinho (pronounced 'shree vinyo') club in Lisbon. Silence suddenly came over the large crowd as a guitarist, standing in the centre of the floor, started to play. A plainly-dressed woman stood by him, and commenced a sad singing in the Fado style. The audience was silent in its emotional grip. The soul of Portugal was laid bare in this unforgettable experience.

This poem was written at a candlelit table, on a table napkin, during her performance.

FADO SINGER

(after a visit to Sr. Vinho Fado Restaurante — Lisbon,
Portugal, April 1983)

Flickering candles pick out a lonely form,
'Neath Sr. Vinho's low-beamed roof in old Lisboa.
So sadly she stands, hands clenched, her head held
high,
Singing her heart out whilst tears run down her face.

Sad deep-throated soulful cry from Lisboa's heart,
A resonant sound that reaches to our souls.
An almost Eastern wailing sad lament,
Perhaps of lovers' heavy hearts and absent friends?

Our spirits feel her strong insistent crying,
To move us all in sympathy she's trying.
Baring her emotions to the flames of living,
A sound of human striving she is giving.

Fado, singer, singer, calling to the night,
I would linger, linger, take a brief respite.
Out there (and here) the sad, sad hearts are crying,
But Fado voice is strong though times are trying.

ALGARVE FLOWER

This poem is dedicated to an elderly English lady,
Dorothy, who lived and died in the Algarve. She died
just before Easter. She was 'thoroughly English', true to
her country and its traditions and culture.
   She is likened to the wild-white Iris of the Algarve.

ALGARVE FLOWER

(March 1983)

This wet but sunny time brings varied flowers,
Sprinkling the hills and vales with many hues.
I stopped by winding roadside steep to view,
Tall wild-white Algarve Iris quite profuse.

Oh! pretty flower in hilly wild terrain,
Tall, green and hardy, topped with petals white.
Six outer, curly petals, three inside,
Three pollen-bearing golden furry tongues.

This Easter time the Iris stands upright,
As though it was the cross that bore His frame.
It's whiteness, the purity of His life,
Its dying at this time, His pregnant death.

Easter bells, chiming clear across the world,
Ringing, singing their word of hope in hearts.
The joyful heart of Jesus reaches here,
Filling the Algarve with His Easter cheer.

For one who lived as bravely as she died,
And never made a show of her beliefs.
For one who lived her life to full extent,
Sweet Algarve flower will quietly speak each year.

Pretty, oh! very pretty Algarve flower,
Sweet tall white Iris of this sunny land.
You'll soon be gone but joy you've given us —
We're glad you've made provision to return.

ALBUFEIRA

A popular resort in the Algarve — a haven for
sunbathers, and my first port of call in Portugal after a
long absence.

It was VERY hot!

Some visitors to Albufeira seek the shade, cool cafés
and cool drinks. The poet is surprised to see the sun
worshippers lying day in, day out, on the beaches, in the
scorching sun.

It felt as though Albufeira was punishing him for
staying away so long? (if he had visited frequently, the
heat would not seem so threatening!)

Although one of the shorter poems delivered at the
Riverside Studios performance, this was 'sensational', due
to a brilliant delivery by an actress complete with sun hat
and sunglasses! . . . a show stopper, in Lancashire dialect.

ALBUFEIRA
(1985)

(The Algarve on a hot Saturday)

A bumpy 'bus takes us to oven town,
Two short, smart policemen stand in heated square.
Steep, narrow streets make walking weary work,
To gain a view of golden strand below.

Hundreds of prostrate worshippers lie there,
This is the magnet pull that draws them all.
From poles apart with languages diverse,
And there they lie and play in heated pan.

It's a pleasant town for all the crush,
With pretty bars away from draining heat.
Market stalls' mouth-watering melons,
Seep with juice when they are sliced in two.

Have I been chided by hot southern land,
For my long absence from its soil of golden brown?
I dragged my weary feet back to my place —
The burning Sun had sapped my strength away.

ESTOI RE-VISITED

The ruins of a small Roman town, near Faro in the Algarve (the Roman town of Ossonoba). It is a small settlement with Temple, Baths and living quarters, on a beautiful, sunny plain.

I always feel haunted by Roman ghosts in such towns.

This place holds lovely memories for me, and its compactness is attractive.

ESTOI RE-VISTED

(Milrieu, near Faro in the Algarve)
The Roman town of Ossonoba ICAD — 1985

I had to feel you Roman ghosts again,
I had to join you in the temple hall.
Golden Roman town of Ossonoba,
In fertile blue-sky'd southern sunny land.

Draw aside (in mind) in temple's coolness,
Hush! can you hear the song and music there?
The temple stands austere and yet inviting
'Gainst sun-bathed backdrop, bright-blue, green and red.

Pools with polychrome mosaic facing,
Splashing, shimmering waters, oh! so cool.
Paradise on Earth for weary travellers,
Grateful centurion cools his aching limbs.

Can you hear their earnest talk in steam baths?
And splashing waters of the swimming pool?
Leave them to their massage benches comforts,
And childrens' voices sing around the well.

If only I'd been here in Roman times,
In morning light I'd look up to the hills.
And then I'd thrill to stirring of the town,
To cries of children and bark of dog.

Tired-looking, iron-faced sentries changing watch,
As southern golden Sun breaks o'er the plain.
Its brilliant rays pick out the temple front,
And early-risers gather round the well.

A FIRST VISIT TO SPAIN

A very special emotional experience — relating to a short dash into Spain from Portugal in the intense heat of high Summer.

A vivid experience of a Sun-drenched land and its culture. The journey starts at the church in the walled town of Silves ('Silvesh'), in the Algarve, then to Vila Real de San Antonio, over the water to the Spanish town of Ayamonte, then to Sevilla.

Experiences in the great City, including a flamenco club in the cool of the evening, and the great cathedral in the rising heat of the morning. Then the return to Ayamonte and back into Portugal. It was my very first, exploratory visit, and I yearned to return.

A FIRST VISIT TO SPAIN
(1981)

SILVES (The Monchique — Algarve)

I lit a candle in a far-off place,
Faint-warming flame soft-flickered in my face.
Walled town's church, so-cool refuge from the Sun —
I sought your lovely face my precious one.

VILA REAL de SAN ANTONIO (looking across to Spain)

Distant glimpse of time-mellowed sunny land,
In early morning's gentle warming hand.
Modest little town cupped us in its palm,
By gentle passage over waters calm.

AYAMONTE (on arrival in Spain)

Intense morning heat bore down upon me,
Proud young policeman strutted in the square.
Ticket office yielded secrets slowly,
Of chariot bound for proud Sevilla fair.

Field upon field, hot flat-plains unfolding,
Such neat Spanish fields, bathed in white sunlight.
White walled town, neat-perched on a low hill,
Shimmers in heat and speaks out from the past.

Into hot Huelva, our coach nosed briefly,
(time for an ice cream to combat my thirst).
Then hot brown wide fields flitted and shimmered,
Sevilla unfolded in evening's heat.

SEVILLA

Heat poured out from pavements and buildings,
I walked very slowly, seeking the shade.
Memory of Carmen — startling white bullring,
Into the cool of a Spanish hotel.

Then to the night life of old Sevilla,
La Trocha's flamenco-treasure was found.
Spirit caught up in swirlings and clackings,
And stirred by the singer's fiery heart call.

In early morning's dull-rising heat wave,
I sought the cathedral's shade and cool rest.
Words cannot describe the stony immenseness —
And cool pressing silence oozed from its walls.

Here was the heart of the great ancient city,
Here was the faith of a people so proud.
Speak to us, too, who share not the substance,
Strengthen our faith in the purpose of life.

So-brief encounter, Sevilla my city,
Alcazar promised such future delights.
Rushed to the station to leave sweet Sevilla,
Quaint little train moves so slowly away.

Part of my heart was left in Sevilla,
It touched on my soul in numerous ways.
Soaked in its beauty, bathed in its sunshine,
Touched by its culture — I'll go back some day.

RETURN TO AYAMONTE

Spanish old lady, dressed-over in black,
Sat in my carriage, impassive lined face.
Hardship and sorrow-constant companions,
Buttressed by faith and belief in her God?

Neat little craft manoeuvred from quayside,
Ayamonte and Spain slipped slowly away.
Amongst all the chatter I looked back in silence,
Could so much pleasure be felt in two days?

SKETCHES FROM ALCAZAR DE SEVILLA

The exquisite, ancient Moorish palace in Sevilla. Next to the great Cathedral ... and the beautiful white-walled Jewish quarter.

A place of great peace.

It summons up the olden times of Moorish rule and culture. It is said to have been modelled on the great Palace of the Alhambra at Granada, and there are indeed strong similarities.

I sat by a small fountained pool in the courtyard before entering the Palace and its gardens, and that is where the poem starts.

SKETCHES FROM ALCAZAR DE SEVILLA
(April 1983)

I
OUTSIDE COURTYARD

(to be read very quietly and slowly)

Seven potted plants sit round tiny pool,
Some sweet purple flowers bloom, the others wait.
Gentle curving fountain falls and patters,
Inside clear water surface marbled ring.

Pitter-patter, pitter-patter, tinkle
Sound, split and splat, spit and splash, peaceful
sound.
Soft invites your spirit to be tranquil,

Brings sweet comfort to your troubled mind.

II
THE PALACE

A Moorish complex window lets in light,
Through leafy trees that filter sunlight rays.
Shade upon shade of hazy sunny greens,
The complex window lattice helps the theme.

134

I lean on cool sill close to window old,
And look out through a square-on-square design.
A close secluded garden in the sun,
I think of tearful arab lovers' eyes.

An ancient Moorish courtyard in the Sun,
Soft stone elegance of fretted pillars.
Round about, a sea of tiny coloured tiles,
Above, white balcony of many sighs.

III
GARDENS

What can I say of Alcazares gardens?
Sweet heavy scents the senses overwhelm.
Palm trees tower ... not in unseemly pride,
Fitting like glove into the varied greens.

Top-heavy, odd shaped trees of desert sands,
Speak more to *me* than all — of Moorish kings.
Bringing to Sevilla's sunny plain,
Ambassadors from land of Arab dreams.

The palm tree's bark has wizened, crinkly look,
Wrapped all about with stringy, clinging vines.
Tiny gold growing juicy spheres on tree,
That arches, oh! so gracefully below.

Unobtrusive orange tree bears rich fruits,
Quite small and brightly coloured at this time.
And there! you see a bush of different spheres,
Made up of green-white petals so profuse.

Cactus, flat-green and spiky thing by wall,
You are a strange bedfellow here, I feel.
You are at home in even sunnier climes,
You'll laugh and sing where other plants would die.

Thick, bent and ugly solid pimply trunk,
And many pale green spiky flat-pod leaves.
I could expect you on a planet bleak,
But you are firm-established here.

EPILOGUE

Waft, waft Sevilla's cooling evening breeze,
Waft heady perfumed air to senses keen.
Sing and twitter, warbling pretty birds,
I'll say goodbye again with senses stirred.

SEVILLA CATHEDRAL

An amazing building: when they first discussed its possibility, they said 'let us build such an edifice that men in future generations will say that 'they were mad' ' (to attempt it)!

The poem is an attempt to describe its immensity and beauty of form — and its spiritual atmosphere.

When first entering from the inevitable, blinding Sevillian sunshine — the cathedral seems to be totally black inside.

As the eyes become accustomed to the new environment — great wonders unfold.

It is truly a 'wonder of the world'. Its Moorish Giralda Tower looks down on a main thoroughfare of Sevilla, on the one side the Jewish Quarter, and on another, the Palace and its gardens.

SEVILLA CATHEDRAL

(Easter 1983)

The entrance to this ancient place streams light,
Filtering rays of sunlight meet the dark.
An ancient heavy door 'neath vaulted roof,
Frames a clear blue Sevilla sky and square.

I turn around and view a darker place,
So-high roof above, on columns fluted.
Such strange depths of peaceful half-light darkness,
Two high stained windows glow with coloured light.

To left, roof upon vaulted roof appear,
Unfolding in a rolling sea of stone.
Wrought iron gilded gatework reaches upward,
Towards a multi-windowed complex roof.

This piece of roof o'er massive sculptured gates,
Fans out from base in sweeping gentle curves.
Backcloth for five jewel-like stained glass windows,
Two large, three small, in profuse colour rich.

*****

The richness of the altar takes the eyes,
Silver and gold profusion takes the breath.
The massive walls of complex sculptured forms,
Form upon form of saints and cherubims.

If one can tear the gaze from lower things,
And look up to the lightful source above.
A lofty dome is seen with central light,
And radial sculptures o'er elliptic form.

138

Soft candlelight and filtered sunlight joined,
A bank of flick'ring candles in the haze.
They speak out, plead perhaps for substance real,
Midst the tramp of tourists' feet and chatter.

*****

A smooth light-mottled marble front,
With four pillars and gilded doors.
Supports the organ's silver tubes,
Framed with sharp figures carved in wood.

From here, above, to right and left,
High roofs abound to take the breath.
Great windows catch the sun's bright glare,
A hole shoots pool of light to floor.

Look up to source of pencil light,
Its blinding glare blanks all else out.
Ellipse of light upon the floor,
Shimmers like tiny water pool.

Young girl from USA stopped by,
Called to her friend to come and look.
'Say, Angeline!' (she said), 'what's *this*?'
Brief moment and they went away.

*****

EPILOGUE

A chiming bell reminds me of the time,
And I must really tear myself away.
Once more from place of memories so sweet,
Once more approach the door to sunbathed square.

MERIDA

An amazingly preserved major Roman Ruin near Badajoz, close to the border between Spain and Portugal. It has an incredibly preserved Amphitheatre and Theatre. It stirred deep feelings of the Roman presence.

The site revived the writer's amazement at the paradox of Roman civilization.

On the one hand, the cruelty of the Amphitheatre, and on the other hand the deep interest of Romans in the theatre and law.

In the space below the Amphitheatre floor I saw iron rings still embedded in the walls — and imagined the terrors of prisoners waiting there, shackled, until their turn came to be killed in the arena.

MERIDA

ROMAN RUINS — Merida, near Badajoz (Spain)-
April 1983 re-structured August 1984

AMPHITHEATRE

The greedy, heady roar of callous crowds,
And snarls of angry beasts that prowled and died.
Men fighting beasts and men, oft' times to death —
Did many christians die an ugly death?

The heat and stench below the arena floor,
Are more than I can bear — I clutch my throat.
And, shackled, press against the stony wall,
As snapping, snarling beasts are dragged close by.

Brilliant sunlight streams through grill above,
The muted roars of inflamed crowds seep through.
A headless lion drops through opened trap,
And blood runs past my feet in narrow trough.

THEATRE

It is a warm and clear-skied Spanish night,
And Roman actors walk the stony stage.
Quietness falls o'er the crowded theatre floor,
Hush! can't you hear the instrumental sounds?

I stood upon the stage and cast my voice,
And it was caught within the ring of stone.
Roman voices pierced the still night air and
Gripping tales cast spells as plots unfold.

LIVING AREA

A colony of ants at busy work,
Pouring o'er stony ledge and to a hole.
I watch one pull a reed five times its size!
Across and down the rock and over ground.

Fierce little hurrying, black Spanish ants,
So busy collecting remnants of plants.
No doubt your progenitors worked this ground,
Where many sandalled Roman feet were found.

EPILOGUE

The world has changed, and changed, and Rome has
gone,
And modern man has moved on fast in pride.
He fears he has the seed of his own doom,
Ants will be here, I guess, when man has gone?

I walk slowly from the haunting ruins,
I hear (I'm sure) the amphitheatre's roar.
Music and actors' voices ringing out,
Like sirens calling from an awesome age.

I feel a dogged haunting of my steps,
The Romans call and jest and bother me.
Our age bears many imprints of their law,
The framework of our language bears their stamp.

Soft-snuggled on this Spanish plain,
In Spanish evening sunlight's warming glow.
Merida holding history in its hand,
Unsettling glimpse of Roman life in Spain.

Oh! Roman spirits, do not haunt me so,
I'd leave Merida's ancient walls in peace.
Unhand me! spirits of a bygone age!
Break loose your hold for I must go away.

ESCORIAL

An immense palace in a village! Between Segovia and
Madrid. It was a Good Friday, and I sat in the great
church as the service was coming to an end. An intense
experience, of a remarkable male voice choir and intense
evening light beaming down from the high, white dome.
This brief poem was written during the church service
before the atmosphere was lost — nothing should be
added, I believe.

ESCORIAL

(Castile, Spain, April 1982)

Escorial! Escorial! I sat below a dome
So high and white and lighted by the evening Sun.
I knew now why I'd journeyed far from home,
To Sun-bathed plains and hills of old Castile.

Golden tones of choir seemed to enfold me,
The rising notes met up with light diffused.
Below the magic light, twin pulpits stood,
All wrought in gold — with fretted canopies of gold!

I left the town as evening shadows fell,
The magic choral notes still lingered on.
Hot-baked but snow-topped mountains cast against
Escorial's white-walled, clear-cut magic form.

NOTE:

There is a Spanish translation of this poem, by
Manuel Torreras Jimenez (Cordoba)

A CROSS IN SAN LORENZO DEL ESCORIAL

Although quite widely travelled in Spain, I had not seen the breathtaking monument to the Fallen of the Civil War. It is the Santa Cruz del Valle de Los Caidos, fifty eight kilometres north of Madrid.

A little before reaching the town of Guadarrama and after crossing the bridge over the river of the same name, you turn left towards El Escorial and come to the entrance to the Valle, about eight kilometres further on. The grandeur of the Monument and its surrounding buildings catch the eye immediately.

A wild rocky valley with distinctive cone-shaped crag of bare rock at its extremity.

The Monument was ordered to be erected by a decree issued in 1940, and the work was completed in 1958.

An enormous cross (150 metres high) sits on the crag of rock mentioned, and beneath it, the centre of the crag was excavated to accommodate an enormous marbelled Crypt, including a church with great dome — all within the rock.

Anyone familiar with the anguish of the Civil War will feel strongly when confronted by this monument.

Further reading of the history of the Civil War revealed the tragedy of the use of prisoners after the War was over, to work in forced labour on various construction projects, including this one. Tens of thousands of Republican veterans were to perform years of hard labour, and many suffered privation and many died.

The poem is intended to be an anguished cry to the Spanish people to build a united Spain. Near the end of the poem, a deceased political prisoner (who died whilst working on the construction of the monument in the harsh mountain Winter) speaks out to us.

146

A CROSS IN SAN LORENZO DEL ESCORIAL

(May 1988)

In San Lorenzo del Escorial,
North of the Guatel river's winding course.
Above the road that runs from famed Escorial,
To Guadarrama and La Salana,
You'll see a rocky valley touched with green.
Rich pines and oaks, junipers and broom:
Quiet poplars hide in sheltered corners,
Holm-oaks and holly lie amongst the brambles.
Austerity of marjoram and thyme,
Match well with raw Guadarrama range.

Santa Cruz del Valle de Los Caídos,
Beneath your stony warning finger grey,
The tortured cliffs are pierced to mortal wound,
To death, as was the Saviour featured there,
In massive sculptured form — recumbent Christ,
Head raised on Holy Mother Mary's arm.
España's new-birth signified in stone,
A dual resurrection here implied?

It stands, a cross of grey and solid stone,
Upon the mass of solid rock beneath.
Rests heavy on the awesome Crypt below,
And heavier on the tortured soul of Spain.
The Valley of the Fallen's stony finger points
To Spanish passers by, lest they forget
A Nation nearly rent apart in War.

Pass through the mighty doors and wrought-iron
grill,
And walk down stone-and-marble lofty Crypt.
Eight tapestries, each near-nine metres long,
Worked in precious metals, wool and silk,
Record John's Patmos Revelation dream.
And then the mosaic ceiling of the Dome,
Captures the eyes in blaze of myriad coloured tiles.

See! from a viewpoint Station of the Cross,
The awesome Cross grows up from cone-shaped crag.
Grows from the earth that held the Fallen Dead —
Earth stained with blood of patriotic Souls.
Santa Cruz del Valle de Los Caídos,
A lonely rocky sentinel that will not go away,
Deep-anchored to the rocky cliff,
To rest deep-rooted in España's Soul.

******

"I did not think that I for it should die —
Long after bloody War had ceased to rage.
Back-breaking work had bowed me low,
And bitter winds had pierced me through.
Deep-cut skin of hands and broken nails,
Oh! sharp, hard Guadarrama rocks!
I did not think that I would ever hate
A monument so vast in concept and design."

The shadow of the stony finger falls,
On those in Spain who lose the vision clear:
One Nation strong! — the finger points
To patriots who, in desperate quest
To rule themselves, lose sight of all the Dead
Gave up to win — A NEW UNITED SPAIN.
Leaders and Youth of Spain must feel
Its drawing, driving force —
OR ALL HAS BEEN IN VAIN.

NOTE:

There is a Spanish translation of this poem, by
Manuel Torreras Jimenez (Cordoba)